A KID'S HERB BOOK

by

LESLEY TIERRA

Illustrations by Susie Wilson
Foreword and Original Songs by Michael Tierra
Design by Marge Ann Wimpee

Robert D. Reed Publishers

Robert D. Reed Publishers
P.O. Box 1992
Bandon, OR 97411
(541) 347-9882
E-mail: 4bobreed@msn.com
Website: www.rdrpublishers.com

Art, design, production, and manufacturing under the direction of
Dane Petersen, Petersen Books, a division of Double Eagle Industries.
For manufacturing details, call 831-204-7770.
E-mail: dane@petersenbooks.com

Illustrations by Susie Wilson - Foreword and Original Songs by Michael Tierra

Edited by Katherine Hyde - Typesetting by Marge Ann Wimpee

Thirteenth printing 2022

ISBN 978-1-885003-36-2

Library of Congress Catalog Number: 99-067463

Dedication

To my son, Chetan, now a young man of 16.

May this bring you, your children, and your children's children great fun from the projects and songs, wisdom from the stories and healing knowledge from the herbs.

A KID'S HERB BOOK

For Kids of All Ages

Table of Contents

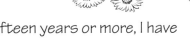

Thanks

Since the writing of this book has spanned a good fifteen years or more, I have many people to thank:

Michael Tierra, for your inspiration, profound herbal wisdom, encouragement and astute feedback on this work. Thank you also for your delightful songs and creative improvements on "Fluffy Cloud"!

Chetan Tierra, my son, whose constant requests for bedtime stories in his early years kept my imagination alive and active. It is for you that I originally wrote this book. And thanks for your original idea for the story, "The Evil Phantom."

Bonnie Gunsaulus, my wonderful mother, whose love of literature sparked my own—many thanks for your repeated patient reading, insightful editing, delight in my stories and boundless belief in me.

Richard, Mary Jane, Megan and Colleen Gunsaulus, my brother, sister-in-law and nieces, for your fabulous insights, wonderful suggestions and great editing input.

Susie Wilson, for your beautiful illustrations and devoted support of this project.

Marge Ann Wimpee, for your incredibly skillful and creative layout designs.

Beau and Justin Agnello, although not born at the beginning stages of this herbal, are now wonderful listeners to these stories. Your suggestions and ideas have been marvelous and have helped shape the content of this work. And thanks to mom, **Jill Agnello,** for your support in this work.

Marjorie Wolfe, for your endless patience and encouragement while typing and retyping this constantly changing manuscript. And thanks for naming Ginglegrink in the story, "Ginger, the Golden Root"!

Nina Paulson, for your work in repeatedly helping to get manuscript copies together.

Aviva Romm and Becky Shields, for your generous editing input.

Lisa and Kate Barber, my old friend and her daughter, for your professional and invaluable editing ideas.

Nora Martin and Roy Upton, for your wise professional suggestions and willing help.

Sally Wise and her son, Jamal, for your detailed editing and insightful feedback.

Ellen Bass, my encouraging writing teacher during the inception of this book.

Beth Buerkens, for your infectious laughter and creative ideas.

Darlena Theocharides, Joan Anderson and Diane McCabe, for your everlasting friendship during the writing of this book. Joan, I especially thank you for reviewing the manuscript with "effortless joy" and for your loving comments.

Jeannine Parvati Baker, Gannon, Quinn and the twins, for your encouragement and wonderful editing ideas on the original manuscript.

Ga Lombard at Bookshop Santa Cruz, for your generous and wise guidance in determining the format for this book.

Thanks to the rest of my family—my dad, **Robert Gunsaulus,** for your loving support throughout my life—and to **Jane, Lee, Lesley, Noel and Nancy Weisenbach,** my sister, brother-in-law and nieces, for your contagious humor and playfulness.

Foreword

After completing the first edition of *The Way of Herbs* many years ago, my wife, Lesley, proposed that I write an herb book for young kids. With many projects before me, I never got to this one and soon Lesley realized that if it was to be done, perhaps she should do it herself. Eager to combine her creative talents as a children's storywriter with her vast knowledge of herbs, this book has finally come to manifestation. As such, it is to date the first herb book for children.

We both feel that the seeds planted in youth are those whose roots go the deepest. I remember how my Italian parents always designated a small garden plot that was solely mine to grow and tend various seeds. I never forgot the vegetables, pansies and snapdragons I grew, and I became quite proud of my ability to grow roses from cuttings. Considering my life that followed through the range of being a classical musician, choral conductor, composer, father, beatnik, Haight Ashbury hippie and then living in a wilderness community in Northern California, I became closer each time to the garden of my youth. Finally, now living in the mountains of Santa Cruz, California, surrounded by a garden that is far too big for me to manage and maintain alone, I can see how the seeds of childhood eventually manifested in my life.

I say this not so much to tell about myself, but rather to reassure parents everywhere that there is profound and lasting value to that which we take the time to introduce to our young children. Probably the actual plot given to me for my childhood garden was not more than a few feet in diameter, but it is strange how large the seemingly small things of childhood become in the memories of our maturity.

Throughout recent history herbal medicine has been practically eclipsed by so-called modern techno-medicine. Yet, because of a profound need for a safer, more natural and harmonious medicine I, along with a handful of other colleagues since the late 60's, have been able to revitalize what is perhaps one of the most ancient arts of all, the art of herbal medicine. It has been a colorful and wonderful journey, but both Lesley and I agree that if it is to continue into the 21st century and beyond, we must share our love of healing plants with children beginning at the youngest possible age.

I believe that it is our calling as parents to share the things we love and believe in with our children. To say that we love our children bears a responsibility of spending such quality time with them, especially in those vitally important early formative years. It is to this intention that Lesley's book is offered.

Michael Tierra
Author of *The Way of Herbs* and *Planetary Herbology*

Introduction

Over fifteen years ago I embarked on the journey of writing this book. At the time my husband, Michael Tierra, had started writing a children's herbal. It consisted of an idea, a list of possible herbs, and several herb songs. I loved the concept and kept waiting for Michael to complete it. But, because he was involved in so many other projects, he never did. Finally, it occurred to me to write the children's herbal myself. I had contributed several ideas and developments to Michael's original concept and carried forth the vision while waiting on him. Why not do it myself?

I sent the completed work to a dozen major publishers. All my responses were the same. The book was a great concept and was well written, but it fell in a crack between the ages: it was too mature for children and too young for adults. Thus, it wasn't satisfactory for either. That's when I decided to divide the work in two, creating an adult herbal and a children's herbal. The adult herbal was published first through Crossing Press in 1994 under the title, **The Herbs of Life.** Then I turned my attention to this, the children's herbal.

Over the years my concept and vision of this work have continuously changed. It has gone through a careful refining process to reach this final form. In a way, I felt it guiding me, as if it had taken on a life of its own. It has been fun, satisfying and a great creative outlet.

In guiding children to use this book, be sure to point out the glossary of herbal terms near the end. Both definitions and pronunciation of general herbal terms are given there. The appendices also hold useful information for children and adults to know as they use this book. Appendix 2 covers dosages for children, while Appendix 5 lists several useful resources for enhancing the herbal learning process. Further, Appendix 3 includes a detailed list of common ailments and their herbal remedies. Hopefully this book will also provide children and adults with a simple guide to begin healing themselves.

I truly believe nature is a great healer through her many gifts of minerals, plants, animals and many other things, as well as through her great beauty. There is much that is still a mystery about this planet we call home. May this book nurture children, inspiring them to explore nature, awaken to the healing power of herbs and become active in preserving our natural environment.

A Few Notes to Adults:

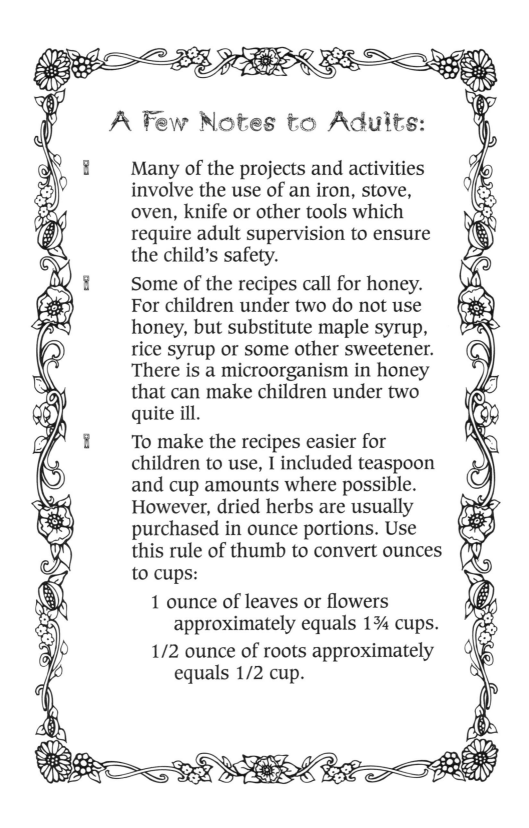

- Many of the projects and activities involve the use of an iron, stove, oven, knife or other tools which require adult supervision to ensure the child's safety.

- Some of the recipes call for honey. For children under two do not use honey, but substitute maple syrup, rice syrup or some other sweetener. There is a microorganism in honey that can make children under two quite ill.

- To make the recipes easier for children to use, I included teaspoon and cup amounts where possible. However, dried herbs are usually purchased in ounce portions. Use this rule of thumb to convert ounces to cups:

    1 ounce of leaves or flowers approximately equals 1¾ cups.

    1/2 ounce of roots approximately equals 1/2 cup.

Hi! My Name Is Mr. Greenleaf!

I'd like to take you on a magical adventure into the wonderful world of herbs! Plants grow all around us. Usually we enjoy their beauty, yet many of them hold special powers as well. Flowers, trees, weeds, even spices for food, can help us feel better or get well from sickness. Would you like to learn about them?

Then follow me page by page through this fun adventure book. I wrote this book for YOU to use and play with. You can follow the activities, do the projects, learn the information, sing the songs, read the stories and even color in all the pictures you want. Plus, if you look closely, you'll find me hiding in many different spots throughout this book. Where's Mr. Greenleaf? Here I am!

Now, don't delay. Turn the page and enter the magical kin-dom of plants!

PLANTS ARE OUR FRIENDS

Plants are extremely important to our lives. Did you know that we couldn't breathe without plants? Plants provide oxygen for the air we breathe. That's one important reason not to cut down too many trees on our earth.

Plants provide our primary source of beauty. When plants die, they fertilize the soil and new plants grow in their places. They give a beautiful and colorful clothing to our planet.

People once used plants for many other purposes. They used shredded bark for clothing, dyes to color clothes or bodies, rope to tame animals and plants for covering dwellings.

Plants give us our food! We eat plants ourselves and the animals we eat (if we eat animals) have eaten plants. Way before there were supermarkets or farms, people picked wild nuts, fruits, berries, leaves and roots of certain plants for food. Many people still do!

Herbs were used for cleaning. For example, if you take a little piece of North American soaproot and rub your hands together in water, it lathers up like soap. Then you can clean your body and clothes with it.

We also get medicines from plants. Trees, barks, leaves, flowers, seeds, berries, grains and roots are all used for healing or nourishment. When used in this way, they are called herbs.

Plants Provide...

- oxygen
- food
- beverages
- clothing
- soap
- dyes
- perfume
- straw
- cork
- rubber
- wood
- paper
- cotton
- medicines

MAKE A NATURAL TOOTHBRUSH

Did you know that you can use a plant as your toothbrush and toothpaste? People throughout the world have used plants to keep their teeth clean and gums healthy. It is still one of the best methods to clean our teeth, since tree twigs are filled with substances that strengthen our gums and protect them from infections.

To make your own natural toothbrush: Pick a smooth twig from the branch of a non-poisonous tree. In India they use the neem tree. One of my favorites is the bay laurel tree. Chew on the end until the strands separate a bit, like a small tooth-brush. Now rub it on your gums and around your teeth. Does your mouth feel tingly and clean afterwards?

Tree twigs to use: Bay, eucalyptus; licorice sticks can be purchased at the health food store and work well, too.

CAUTION: Some bushes and trees, such as oleander and yew, are poisonous. Before you use any plant, be sure to have an adult properly identify it as safe.

FLORA OR FAUNA?

lora is plant life. Fauna is animal life. In this book we are studying flora, or plant life, especially plants used for healing.

How old are plants?

How many years would you guess plants have existed on the earth? 500 years? 1000 years? 5000 years?

Plants are more ancient than that. They have been on earth much longer than animals or humans. Club mosses grew 250 million years ago. Cone-bearing shrubs (conifers), such as pines, first grew 150–200 million years ago. Believe it or not, these same types of plants still grow on earth now. In fact, some chaparrals alive today are thousands of years old.

Honor Thy Flora!
Did you know that every state has a special flower and tree that it calls its 'own'? What is your state flower? Your state tree? (**Hint:** Look it up in Appendix 4 at the back of this book.)

By any other name...

How many names do you know for plants? Plants have many different names according to the type of plant it is. Some names include: weed, herb, wort, grass, flora, bush, shrub, tree, flower, fruit, vine, vegetable and spice.

What is an herb?

Any plant used for healing is called an herb. Wouldn't it be interesting to know how a flower, tree or plant can be used to prevent sickness and help you feel better? Different plant parts are used for healing: leaves, flowers, stems, roots, seeds, fruit, grains, tree bark and twigs.

How many herbs do you already know? Check off the ones you know: ✔

❏ borage flower and leaf
❏ loquat fruit and leaf
❏ nettle leaf
❏ thyme leaf

❏ *licorice root*
❏ chrysanthemum flower

❏ *yarrow leaf*
❏ comfrey leaf

❏ *cinnamon bark*
❏ lavender flower
❏ marshmallow leaf
  and root
❏ malvae leaf
❏ lemon balm leaf
❏ honeysuckle flower
❏ magnolia bud

❏ *garlic clove*
❏ red clover flower

❏ *ginger root*
❏ dandelion root and leaf

❏ *fennel leaf and seed*
❏ mustard seed
❏ cayenne pepper

❏ *slippery elm bark*
❏ coneflower
❏ mullein leaf
❏ rose petal
❏ chickweed leaf

❏ *chamomile flower*
❏ plantain leaf
❏ violet flower and leaf

❏ *elder flower and berry*
❏ sage leaf

❏ *calendula flower*
❏ basil leaf

What is a weed?

What is the difference between an herb and a weed? We usually call any plant that is growing where we don't want it to grow a weed. Some grow on our lawns, others in sidewalk cracks or in our vegetable gardens.

Many weeds are actually very useful plants and are used as herbs. Several weeds that we pull out of our gardens are also used for healing. For example, dandelion, plantain and thistle are all "weeds" that are also important herbs.

How many of these so-called weeds do you know? Check them off: ✔

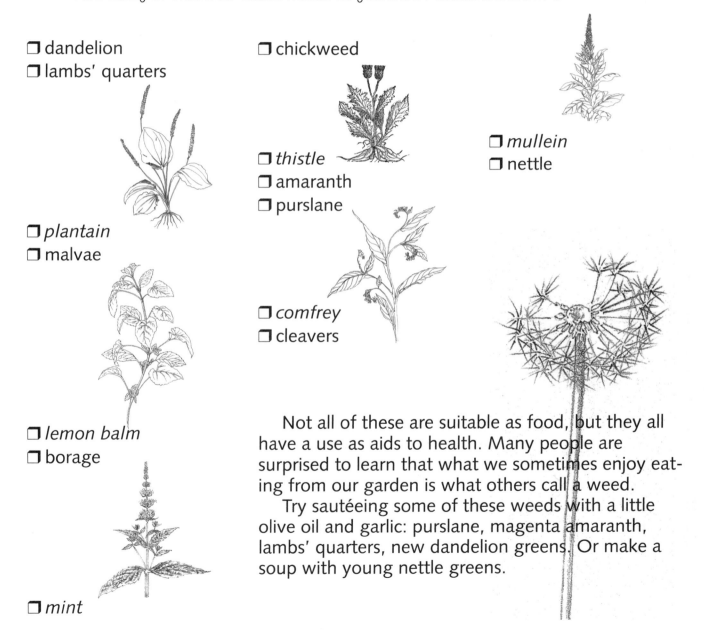

❏ dandelion
❏ lambs' quarters

❏ *plantain*
❏ malvae

❏ *lemon balm*
❏ borage

❏ *mint*

❏ chickweed

❏ *thistle*
❏ amaranth
❏ purslane

❏ *comfrey*
❏ cleavers

❏ *mullein*
❏ nettle

Not all of these are suitable as food, but they all have a use as aids to health. Many people are surprised to learn that what we sometimes enjoy eating from our garden is what others call a weed.

Try sautéeing some of these weeds with a little olive oil and garlic: purslane, magenta amaranth, lambs' quarters, new dandelion greens. Or make a soup with young nettle greens.

What is a spice?

Herbs are also used to spice food. A spice is a plant used for flavoring in cooking. Spices usually have strong tastes and odors. They flavor food so it tastes good. Besides flavoring food, spices also have health-giving properties and can be used for medicine.

How many spices do you know? Check them off: ✔

❒ basil leaf
❒ thyme leaf
❒ oregano leaf

❒ *cayenne pepper*
❒ black peppercorn
❒ mustard seed

❒ *fennel seed*
❒ anise seed
❒ celery seed
❒ dill seed
❒ cumin seed

❒ *ginger root*
❒ cardamom seed
❒ nutmeg seed

❒ *bay leaf*
❒ coriander seed
❒ rosemary leaf
❒ marjoram leaf
❒ sage leaf
❒ caraway seed

❒ *garlic bulb*
❒ turmeric root

⊕UCH!
PLANTS HAVE FEELINGS, TOO!

Just like humans and animals, plants also have feelings. Scientists researched this by placing electrical diodes on plant leaves. Whatever the plants felt was then drawn on a graph. The scientists found that what people said, thought and did affected the plants. Even different types of music affected how well they grew.

If something happened the plants liked, they thrived and the graph looked calm. If something happened to disturb or hurt the plants, the graph picture went wild.

You can read more about these studies in the book, *The Secret Life of Plants* by Peter Tompkins and Christopher O. Bird.

WHAT IS AN HERBALIST?

Any person who uses plants for healing, or who studies herbs very seriously, is called an herbalist.

Do you know any herbalists? List their names here.

_____

_____

_____

_____

If you don't know any herbalists in your community, find one! Go to your local nursery or health food store and ask the people who work there for names of local herbalists. Then visit or interview them.

How did people first learn about herbs?

Have you ever wondered how people first learned how herbs heal?

People learned how to use plants through many ways. The Native Americans learned by watching animals and the plants they ate when they were sick. They especially studied the habits of bears. Native people followed the bears and watched them. When bears are sick, they eat particular plants that help them get well again.

The Native Americans also watched the deer. When deer are injured, they hide in boggy areas and cover themselves with the wild sphagnum moss that grows there. We now know that this moss is a natural healing plant that stops infections.

We can make similar observations. Have you ever noticed how every once in a while your dog and cat like to eat green grass and then throw it all up? This is a natural cleaning method your pets use to keep themselves healthy. (Of course, not all plants that animals eat are safe for people. Deer eat poison ivy berries, but that wouldn't be too good for us humans!)

These observations were passed down over a long period of time until they formed the many rich herbal traditions that still exist throughout the world.

DID YOU KNOW . . .

Most all countries have native traditions about herbs and healing. Here are a few countries that have rich herbal traditions: China, Japan, India, Indonesia, Africa, Mexico, Iran, Iraq and Turkey. Many countries in Europe, Central America and South America also have herbal traditions, as do Native American tribes of North America.

The fun part is that today we can learn from all of them.

The written history of ancient cultures often mentions the use of herbs for healing. It was not until the last century that chemical medicine was largely adopted.

Today, many people throughout the world still use herbs as their main form of disease prevention.

Are all herbs safe?

Some plants are poisonous, like oleander, rhododendron, foxglove and elephant ear. Many people grow these as ornamentals. Other plants cause skin irritations, like poison oak, poison ivy and stinging nettle. (Pick fresh nettles with gloves. When the nettles are cooked they will lose all their sting.) Thus, it is important that you identify and understand plants before using them as herbs. Luckily there are more safe plants than not. NEVER TASTE A PLANT WITHOUT YOUR PARENTS' PERMISSION!

BECOME A PLANT!

Have you ever wondered what it would be like to be a plant? While you can't change into a plant, you can see what it might feel like to be one. To try this, choose any plant that you like and sit in front of it. Make your mind and thoughts as quiet as you can. You can keep your eyes open, or close them if you want.

Now imagine you are very small and sitting on one of the leaves of the plant. Then let yourself slide down the leaf into the stalk of the plant. Imagine the liquid rising up the stalk and any sounds the plant makes as it grows. Feel each stem, leaf and flower stretch and unfold.

Next, imagine that you are entering one of the cells that form the plant's body. Then go all the way down to the roots that reach deep into the earth. Feel the roots drink the water from the soil.

Go back up the stalk and into one of the leaves. Feel the leaves take in the light from the sun. Watch the light and food moving through the various parts of the plant.

How does it feel to be a plant?

NATURAL ROOT BEER

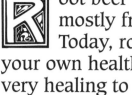

Root beer used to be made only from herbs. It gets its flavor mostly from two of the herbs, sassafras and sarsaparilla. Today, root beer is made from flavored syrup. Make your own healthy root beer at home! The herb, sarsaparilla, is very healing to the liver, blood and skin. Here is one "soda pop" that can clear skin blemishes rather than causing them!

- Simmer 1 tablespoon sarsaparilla in 1½ cups water covered for 15 minutes. Be careful not to let it boil over.
- Add 2 teaspoons anise seeds and ¼ teaspoon cinnamon (bark is best, but you can use powdered, too). Steep covered 10 minutes.
- Strain. Add ¼ cup carbonated water.
- Cool. Drink and enjoy!

MAKE YOUR OWN MARSHMALLOWS!

I'll bet you love marshmallows roasted over a fire during summer or in your hot chocolate in winter. Originally the French boiled marshmallow root to soften it and release its sweetness. Eventually, it turned into the marshmallows we know today which do not contain a trace of marshmallow at all anymore! That's a shame because this white root is very soothing to the skin and heals inflammations in the body. So try making your own marshmallows using the real herb, just as people in France once did.

- Preheat oven to 275 degrees F.
- Separate 2 eggs, keeping the whites. Beat whites until very foamy and not quite stiff.
- Beat in ½ teaspoon vanilla.
- Slowly beat in ½ cup sugar, 1 teaspoon at a time.
- Beat in 2 tablespoons marshmallow root powder.
- Drop mixture using a teaspoonful at a time on the cookie sheet.
- Bake 1 hour.
- Remove from sheet and let cool. Eat and enjoy!
- To store, tightly cover and place in the refrigerator for several days.

Plants have addresses, too

n earth you have an address. It starts as earth, continent, country and then your state, province or other division, and so on. Animals, plants and other living things also have addresses. A Swedish man named Carolus Linnaeus (1707-1778) created the address, or naming system we still use today. This naming or address system is called **Taxonomy**.

Taxonomy sorts living things according to their characteristics. It names living things to show how things are the same and different. A first classification is general. Then it gets pickier and pickier as we group living things into smaller and smaller groups.

We can use taxonomy to give each plant an address. First, the general classification of all living things on Earth is called a **Kingdom**. There are five Kingdoms: *Plantae* (plants), *Animalia* (animals), *Fungi* (like mold, mildew, mushrooms), *Protocilista* (tiny stuff like amoebas) and *Monera* (bacteria). Plants are in the **Plantae** Kingdom.

Next, a **Phylum** divides up the Kingdoms. Phylums are living things that have a common body plan. Now Phylums are divided up into classes and orders. Beyond having a common body plan, things that match in other ways are said to be in the same **Class. Orders** group living things in even more ways.

Families of living things are the same in more ways than not. Plants in the mint family all have a square stem, for instance.

A **Genus** is a subset of a family.

Species is a group of living things that can mate with each other, but have different genes.

Taxonomy names are Latin names. Latin is the common language for names of all life, even humans! (We are *Homo-sapiens* in Latin.) Knowing the special address, or name, of an herb helps identify the right plant, for no other plant has that name. Then whatever language you speak in the world, you are still able to recognize that plant because of its special name.

In French the dandelion is named *Dent de Lion* (meaning 'lion's tooth'). In China it is called *Pu Gong Ying*. But if we use the special name, *Taraxacum officinalis*, everyone knows which single plant in the whole wide world we are talking about, because there is only one *Taraxacum officinalis*. Next time you see a dandelion, try saying, *"Good morning, Taraxacum officinalis!"*

For instance, the special address, or name, of dandelion is *Taraxacum officinalis*:

Kingdom: *Plantae* (plan-tay) This is the plant kingdom.

Division: *Magnoliophytho* (mag-no-lee-ohp-fi-toe) This includes the flowering plants.

Class: *Magnoliopsida* (mag-no-lee-ophp-sea-da) These are the dicots, or plants that have two or more leaves.

Order: *Aster*

Family: *Compositae* (come-pa-si-tay) These flowers have a big head with dozens of petals radiating outward, like a sunflower.

Genus: *Taraxacum* (tear-axe-ah-cum)

Species: *Officinalis* (oh-fish-in-nell-is)

HERBAL LORE

Many stories about the healing powers of herbs have passed down through the ages. They create a body of knowledge called herbal lore. Here is one that is true:

Once in China hundreds of years ago there was a battle between many people. During the battle an old gray-haired general, named He Shou Wu, was captured by the enemy. They took him away and left him to die in a very deep hole in the wilderness. Some people passed by the hole about a year later, expecting to find the skeleton of a dead man. Instead they were amazed to see a very healthy man with his hair fully restored to its youthful color.

The general told them that he had found a plant growing as a weed in the hole. He ate its roots and leaves to stay alive. Not only did the plant keep him well and healthy, but it also turned his gray hair back to its original black color!

People were amazed. Ever since the plant has been used to return hair that turns grey early in life back to its youthful color. They named the plant He Shou Wu in honor of the captured general who discovered it. To this day, the herb He Shou Wu is still used in China.

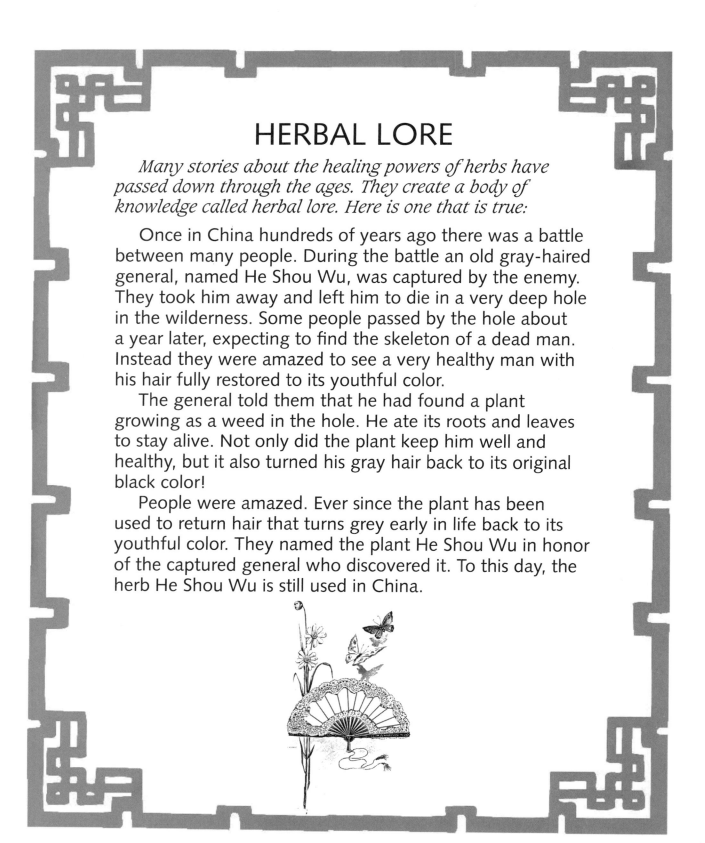

STORY TIME!

Do you like stories? If so, here's one for you
about the magic of herbs. Can you make up a
story about a plant? A favorite flower?
How popcorn was invented?

The Magic Garden

Katie and her younger brother Scott lay sleeping in their beds when suddenly a soft fluttering sound awakened Katie. Outside the glass doors leading to the garden was a giant bird slowly flying in the moonlight. All around its gently flapping wings shimmered the colors of the rainbow. The bird was so beautiful that Katie climbed out of bed, opened the doors and stared breathlessly at the bird.

Just then the bird spoke. "Come, Katie, it is time to go. We have much to do and the moon is already high. Get Scott and hop on. You'll be safe." The bird slowed her flapping wings and landed on the ground outside the glass doors.

Somehow the thought of flying on the bird's back didn't seem strange to Katie. Quickly she woke Scott up and helped him onto the bird in front of her. They had to wiggle around a bit to keep their legs out of the way of the bird's wings. Snuggling close to the bird's neck, they put their arms around its chest and were ready to go.

Silently the bird lifted off and flew high into the dark sky. The bird's colors shimmered on the moonlit clouds, and Katie thought they were riding on a rainbow pathway. Soon the clouds parted and the bird descended. As the bird landed Katie noticed that the sun shone brightly and quiet music could be heard.

"Where are we?" Katie asked excitedly.

"This is the Magic Garden of all plant life," the bird answered. "Follow the blue stone path and when it is time to go, I will find you."

Carefully Katie helped Scott climb off the bird's back and they both watched it fly away. Then gazing at the path before them, they saw the stones were a deep blue with silver specks in them. As she and Scott stepped on each stone it sparkled like the stars in the night sky.

Abruptly Scott pointed and Katie looked up. Amazed, Katie saw that most of the flowers were taller than she was! As they walked along, Katie could look straight into the opened flower petals. There were many plants of all kinds, and each one glowed like a brightly colored light. Yet, although the garden was beautiful, it held a feeling of sadness.

"I wonder why these beautiful flowers feel so sad?" Katie asked out loud.

Suddenly a voice answered. "Sad, humph! You would be sad, too, if you knew what was happening!" Startled, Katie and Scott glanced around but didn't see a single person. The voice came again, only a little louder. "Here I am, right beside you!"

They both looked again and then spotted the largest snapdragon either had ever seen! Each petal was giant, and its colors slowly changed from yellow to orange to red and back to yellow as they looked at it.

"Why yes, I do see you," Katie answered. "But I didn't know that plants could talk!"

"Of course I talk! We all talk! But most humans are too busy to pay attention. If you would look at what is right under your noses you might be surprised at what you can learn, quite surprised indeed." Katie jumped back as the snapdragon's petals snapped together tightly.

Turning to Scott she whispered, "We can hear you talk, but I'm sorry you are not more friendly."

Snapdragon bristled, but looked more closely at Katie. In a softer tone she said, "You are young yet. I've heard that children still believe in us even though adults call it nonsense. Maybe there is still a chance with you."

Hearing a friendlier voice Katie timidly asked, "Please, what do you mean?"

Snapdragon sighed, "Our sister and brother plants on Earth are not loved much anymore. But perhaps you can do something about it. We shall see, we shall see."

"What can I do?" Katie asked, much surprised.

"If you look and listen you will learn," finished Snapdragon. "Now follow the path and pay more attention!"

Katie said good-bye. Taking Scott's hand they quickly walked on. Soon they entered a clearing where clusters of colorful plants were surrounded by pools and fountains.

Katie sighed, "Oh, this is such a beautiful garden!" A light tinkling laughter answered and several tiny white bells caught her eye. Recognizing the plant lily of the valley Katie asked, "Why are you laughing at me?"

Merrily the bells shook and said, "Oh dear us! We are not laughing at you. We are happy that you like us."

Katie watched the tiny bells swing in the breeze and soon began to feel happy, too. Moving closer to the lily of the valley she said, "Now my heart feels really happy."

Lily of the Valley was surprised. "How did you know we are good for your heart? You show more promise than we expected!"

"I didn't know you were good for the heart. I just feel happier being near you" Katie answered.

"But my dear, we are all good for something! We are glad that people enjoy looking at us and smelling us because we do so enjoy giving pleasure. Yet we are more useful than that. Let some of us tell you how."

Katie was curious to hear what they had to say. She and Scott sat down on a large purple and white striped rock. They listened to several plants share their secret gifts.

First, a golden-orange calendula spoke, "I catch the energy of the sun and make you feel warm."

Then Lemon Balm said, "I am cool like the moon so I can lower your fever when you are sick."

Then Dandelion spoke, "I am strong and my root can make you strong, too."

Katie was amazed. "I didn't know you could do all of those things to help people feel better!"

Lily of the Valley sighed. "This may seem new to you, but in the olden days people knew all about us. Oh, it was wonderful then. We were loved not only for our beauty but for our healing powers, too. We are sad because we want to help people and they have forgotten our gifts."

Katie sat quietly for a bit, thinking very hard about what Lily of the Valley and the other plants had said. Suddenly the soft music became louder. Soon Katie heard all the plants singing a hymn of praise together.

"Thanks to the earth which gives us food for our growth. Thanks to the sun that warms us so our seeds sprout with new life. Thanks to the water which satisfies our thirst. Thanks to the air that carries our seeds to new rich lands. We give thanks!"

After a moment a melodic voice sang sweetly, "Children, we are happy you are here listening to our song."

Katie and Scott saw that the rose bush was speaking to them. Its huge rose petals were soft as velvet and filled the air with the sweetest of scents.

Scott touched the majestic rose gently. Katie sighed, "I love this beautiful garden, but I am sad to learn that so many of the plants' gifts have been forgotten."

"This is true," Rose answered. "Yet, there is much that you, Scott and your friends can do to help us."

"I wish that were true, Rose, but we are only children," Katie answered.

A lavender plant across from Katie straightened its purple strands and said, "We need the love of children, Katie."

Near the pond a ginger plant added, "We need children to believe in our healing powers again."

Then Chamomile chimed in, "We need children to help us grow."

Katie never knew that children mattered to plants. She felt very important.

Lemon Balm spoke again, "Love us, and when you want to use us, give thanks before you pick us. This will show that you care about us and love us."

Comfrey explained further, "Remember that the trees, flowers and plants want to help you. Learn about our medicine and use us. Everything in life has a purpose."

Lastly Sunflower said, "Plant more flowers and trees and ask others to plant us too."

Rose broke in, "Children, all you need to do is tell your friends about us and what we have said. Then do these things yourself so that others can learn from you."

Katie was very happy. Now she knew how they could help. "I will do these things, dear plants, and tell my friends, also."

Suddenly a streak of radiant colors flashed overhead. The giant bird was circling above them. Slowly it spiraled down and landed softly on the blue stone path.

"It is time for you to go now, children," Rose said.

Katie noticed that the sadness in the garden was less than before. She was sorry they had to leave. "Will I ever see you again?" she asked.

The plants glowed and spoke all at once, "Katie, we are always with you! We are a part of all the plants you see at home, for we are the spirits of those plants."

The Rose added in her beautiful voice, "Yes, Katie, just remember that the Magic Garden of Plants is real. Off you go now, and may you be blessed."

Katie looked around one last time. She felt happy because she knew that the Magic Garden would always be with her. Holding Scott's hand again, Katie skipped down the path to the giant bird.

As they flew on the back of the giant bird toward their snug beds at home, Katie kept remembering the beautiful magic garden and the things they had been asked to do: love us — use us — plant us — protect us — ask us for our help. With these thoughts, Katie and Scott arrived home and fell soundly asleep.

HERBS OF THE MAGIC GARDEN

Snapdragon - said to calm the nerves but it is hardly ever used. It is best not to use it internally until we know this herb is safe.

Lily of the valley - used by herbalists for heart problems but it can be poisonous so do not use it.

Calendula - used for bruises, scrapes and burns. Fill a small jar with the petals and cover them with olive oil. Set in the sun for 2 or 3 days. Strain the petals and oil through a cloth and squeeze the oil out. What is left is calendula oil. Apply directly to bruises, scrapes and burns.

Rose - used to heal colds and flu. It also helps chase away unwanted sadness and dark feelings.

Lavender - used to scent drawers and closets, it also chases moths away.

Ginger - used for colds. Make a tea and drink at the beginning of a cold.

Chamomile - used for indigestion and stomach aches. Steep 1 teaspoon in a cup of hot water for 10 minutes or so. Drink as is or sweeten with a little honey.

Lemon balm leaves - used as a tea to induce sweating for colds and flu. It also helps chase away unwanted sadness and dark feelings.

Sunflower seeds - used to strengthen your immune system against sickness, as they are rich in Omega 6 fatty acids. They are tasty to eat, toasted or untoasted.

TALKING TO PLANTS

The most obvious ways a plant communicates with us are by where it grows, its appearance, form and color. What do you think a plant with thorns is telling us? Plants such as blackberries, poison oak or poison ivy are called warrior plants because they generally grow in areas disturbed by humans. They do this to make it more difficult for humans to cut them or to protect themselves from being over-harvested. Of course, some people may not admit this, but you and I know, don't we?

How would you like to talk to a plant? Well, here's how. Sit in front of any plant you choose, a tree, herb or flower, for example. Introduce yourself to the plant. Look at it as a very special friend that you want to learn from.

Now close your eyes and take three slow, deep breaths. When you feel ready, ask the plant a question, either out loud, or silently with your mind. Here are some likely questions: How do you grow? Do you need anything right now? Do you like the rain? Do you like the sun? Do you like the shade? What are you used for?

Next, be very still and wait for the plant to answer you. The plant won't talk out loud, of course. Instead, you might hear words in your head like "yes" or "no" or "I need. . .". Let the answers come without disbelieving them. After you get an answer, ask another question, if you wish.

When you are done, be sure to thank the plant for talking with you.

Herb Song

Michael Tierra

2
THE SECRET GIFTS OF HERBS

As you have already seen, herbs have many special gifts. They are like secrets waiting to be discovered. Once you learn the special secrets of each herb, then it is your friend for life.

The herbs included in this chapter are all common and very safe. In fact, most of them either are grown for food or grow as weeds. Also, they are easy to identify once you are familiar with each one. A few of these herbs, such as ginger and cinnamon, only grow in tropical areas.

No matter where you live, there are plants or weeds growing that are usually used as herbs. Look at people's yards, between sidewalk cracks, at potted plants, window box flowers, or at your local nursery. Many of the plants you see there can be used as herbs, too. If you can't find fresh herbs to use, they may be purchased dried in health food stores or even in the spice or produce sections of your local supermarket.

When using fresh herbs, only use those from areas that have not been sprayed with chemicals to kill bugs or weeds. Many supermarkets now have a section of spray-free (called organic) produce. It is also important not to use herbs growing near roads where cars and trucks pass. The reason is that plants absorb the lead from the engine exhaust, and you don't want to use foods and herbs that contain lead! It is always best to eat and use organic herbs and foods whenever possible.

There are not only many secret gifts to learn about herbs, but there are also dozens of fun projects and activities for using them. So what are we waiting for? Let's move on and enter the adventurous, fragrant and fun world of herbs!

LEMON BALM
The Pleasant Fever Breaking Herb

It's hard to think of a more perfect herb for children than lemon balm.

It is easy to grow and has a delicious taste and lemony smell. Lemon balm eases simple colds, coughs and fevers. It is also very relaxing.

Lemon Balm Plant

Green

USE LEMON BALM FOR:

* fevers
* colds, flu
* coughs
* nervousness, whining or crying (for adults, too!)
* wounds and sores

Latin Name: *Melissa officinalis*
Part Used: leaves
Energy and Taste: cool energy; a sour but pleasant taste
Dose for Children: This is a very mild and safe herb. You can drink several cups of the tea a day. For fevers, colds and flu, drink 1/2-1 cup every 2 hours until the fever or cold breaks.
Make as a: tea, tincture, syrup, bath, capsule, sun tea, pill, powder, dream pillow, mouthwash, poultice, potpourri, sachet, salve, steam, foot bath, fomentation, oil.

TOUCH AND FEEL

Feel the stem of a lemon balm plant. Feel for all four sides. Do you feel the square stem?

Pick some lemon balm leaves. Now rub them between the palms of your hands. What do your hands smell like?

Bite off one leaf and chew it. What does it taste like?

42

MAKE A PERFECT CUP OF HERBAL TEA

Imagine sitting by a fire on a cold, blustery day. Wouldn't it be perfect to also sip a cup of warm herbal tea? Of course we don't have to wait for cold days to drink herbal teas. We can have them any time of year.

A medicinal tea is normally made using 1 ounce of herbs to 2 cups of water. There are two ways to make a perfect cup of tea: infusion and decoction.

Infusion is also called steeping. This method is used for delicate, soft leaves, flowers and plants with volatile oils. (Volatile oils are essential oils and they have a strong smell.)

• Bring water to a boil and turn the heat off.

• Put the herbs in a teapot or stainless steel pot.

• Pour boiled water over the herbs in the pot.

• Cover with a lid and let sit 15 minutes.

• Strain the tea and drink.

Decoctions are made by cooking the herbs. This method is used for sturdy coarse leaves, roots, stems, barks and seeds. Cooking the herbs helps to break them down so their medicine seeps into the water. This is called extracting the medicine from the herbs.

• Put the herbs in a stainless steel pot and add water.

• Cover and bring to a boil.

• Simmer for 20–30 minutes.

• Strain the tea and drink.

TEA CONTAINERS
The best containers for making herbal teas are non-metallic, such as glass, earthenware or enamel pots. Stainless steel is all right to use if the others are not available. Whenever possible use spring or purified water, rather than tap water.

USE THE SUN TO MAKE YOUR TEA!

Another way of making an infusion tea is to use the sun. This is called a sun tea.

• Stuff a jar full of your chosen fresh herbs. (Fill the jar 1/4 full of dried herbs.)

• Fill with water and screw on a lid.

• Set in the sun for 6 or more hours.

• Strain.

• Add a little lemon peel or juice, if desired; sweeten to taste.

LEMON ZEST SUN TEA

Lemon balm makes a wonderful summer drink and is much healthier for our bodies than soda. People drank it daily in England during the 16th and 17th centuries because they loved its taste. This yummy tea is great on a hot summer day.

• Stuff a quart jar with fresh lemon balm leaves and flowers. (Fill the jar 1/4 full of dried lemon balm.)

• Squeeze 1 lemon for juice, chop up its peel and add both to the jar.

• Make a sun tea.

• Strain. Add honey to taste.

LEMON BALM TEA

The best way to make lemon balm tea is an infusion. This is because lemon balm has a lot of volatile oils. These oils are what give lemon balm such a wonderful strong odor. Follow the directions for making an infusion, using 1 large handful of fresh lemon balm plants, or 1 teaspoon dried lemon balm for each cup of tea.

CHILDREN'S HAPPY POTION

Do you feel sad or blue? Well, cheer up with the Children's Happy Potion! Lemon balm and chamomile tea is a perfect combination for many children's complaints: restlessness, insomnia, whining, crying, colic, teething, sadness and depression.

To make:

- Infuse 1 teaspoon lemon balm and ½ teaspoon chamomile in 1 cup of water.

- Strain and sweeten to taste.

LEMON BALM, THE HAPPY HERB

Did you know that lemon balm comforts the heart and drives away sadness? It does this by soothing the nervous system, which lifts the spirits. A famous Greek physician, Galen, said that "Lemon balm doth maketh the heart merry." It used to be combined with lemon peel, nutmeg and angelica root for all nervous problems.

45

HERBAL STEAMS

A steam is a method of inhaling fragrant steamy air created from herbs. The herbal steam penetrates your lungs and nostrils, helping to ease your breathing and making you feel better. It is used whenever you have a stuffy nose, lung congestion, allergies, asthma, cough, sinus infection or a cold.

- Make 1 quart tea of your desired herbs.

- While still hot, pour the tea into a very wide pot or bowl, or into a sink or wash basin.

- Put a towel over your head and tuck all the edges in so the steam doesn't escape. Now lean over the pot, sink or basin so your face is near the hot water. (Don't put it too close or you'll burn yourself from the hot tea.)

- Breathe the steamy air for 5-10 minutes or more. Your face will feel hot and wet, but you should start breathing easier and feel better.

- You can also boil 1 quart of water and add 3 drops of an essential oil such as eucalyptus or lavender and use that for your steam.

> **Herbs to use:** lemon balm, thyme, oregano, sage, eucalyptus, mint.

Note: It is important to add into the mix a strong-smelling herb, such as eucalyptus. The strong odor helps to quickly open the sinuses and nasal and lung passages. This allows the other herbs to penetrate more deeply.

RUNAWAY FEVER BREW

Just imagine: lemon balm tea helps us feel well without tasting like medicine! Lemon balm is the very best way to make us sweat. This breaks a fever so it "runs away." At the first signs of a cold, flu or fever, drink a cup of lemon balm tea. Then get dressed warmly and sit or lie down under several covers. Once you start sweating, your fever will break and clear out the cold or flu.

DID YOU KNOW . . .

Lemon balm's name comes from the Greek word meaning "bee." The sweet-smelling oils of the leaves attract bees that in turn produce wonderful honey. The popular name of the oil contained in lemon balm is balsam, which when shortened becomes "balm." Science has discovered that the balsamic oils of plants give off protective ozone that promotes healing and stops infections.

TIME TO GO TO THE OFFICE

The word *officinalis* (oh-fish-in-nal-us) comes from the Latin word *office*. This is because hundreds of years ago the monks and nuns in monasteries were the people who grew and used herbs for the community.

They would catalog and store the herbs in an "office." Then as sick people came to them for healing, the monks and nuns would pull out the appropriate herbs and administer them. They made teas, oils, ointments, balms, syrups, poultices, plasters and other kinds of herbal preparations as well.

If you see the word *officinalis* in the Latin name of an herb, you can be sure it was one of the herbs the monks or nuns used.

Which herbs in this book have the word *officinalis* as part of their names?

SQUARE STEMS!

Can you imagine a plant that has square stems? Actually, many plants do. All plants in the mint family have square stems. Lemon balm is in the mint family.

Story Time!

The Star's Gift

One sunny day, a young girl named Annie decided to make a flower bouquet for her sick mother. Slowly she strolled through the countryside, picking many pretty flowers and wandering farther and farther from home. After a while Annie became very tired. She sat down to rest in the warm sunshine and before long, fell into a deep sleep.

Suddenly Annie awoke at twilight. She jumped up to run home, but didn't know where she was. In the growing dark, everything seemed strange and unusual. She tried finding her way home, but only became more confused and lost. Finally, hungry and worried, Annie sat down and cried.

Soon stars twinkled through the darkness until they filled the night with their glowing light. Now one special star gazed down on the sobbing girl and understood what had happened. The star knew the girl could not find the path by herself at night, so it thought of a way to help her.

Slowly the star shone more and more brightly until it appeared as brilliant as the full moon. Then it sprinkled star-dust down on the lost girl and her path home, creating a trail of silvery light and a beautiful lemony aroma. Annie stopped crying and watched the dazzling shower twinkle like millions of fireflies. She followed the stardust path as if in a dream, never wanting it to end.

When the first streaks of daylight appeared, Annie reached home. Suddenly the stardust trail faded. In its place new plants bloomed, leaving a path of beautiful lemony fragrance. With wonder, Annie realized the star had left the plants as a gift to help her find her way home. She named these plants lemon balm because of their lemony smell and soothing nature. Today this wonderful herb is still around, acting as a balm to sadness and helping us feel happy whenever we drink a tea made from its leaves.

49

Lemon Balm Song

Michael Tierra

FENNEL
Food-Herb That Heals

Fennel is a delicious food that is used as an herb, too. People all over the world eat fennel. It is a rich source of Vitamin A, which keeps the skin healthy and improves eyesight. Fennel seeds are also used by Oriental and European people for a healing medicine.

Fennel Plant

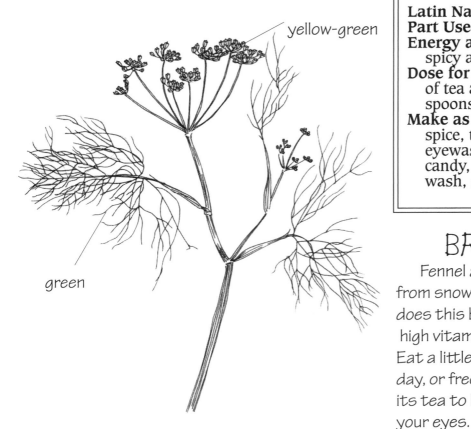

yellow-green

green

USE FENNEL FOR:
* indigestion
* gas
* colic
* nausea, vomiting
* spasms, cramps
* stomach and abdominal pains relieved by heat
* hiccups
* coughs with white mucus
* wheezing, shortness of breath
* decreased appetite
* calming nerves

Latin Name: *Foeniculum vulgare*
Part Used: seeds
Energy and Taste: warm energy, spicy and sweet tastes
Dose for Children: Drink 2 cups of tea a day or eat up to 2 tablespoons of seeds a day.
Make as a: food, potherb, syrup, spice, tea, toothpowder, sun tea, eyewash, pill, powder, capsule, candy, milk, paste, gargle, mouthwash, spice.

BRIGHT EYES

Fennel aids in preventing blindness from snow and bright light reflection. It does this because of its high vitamin A content. Eat a little fennel every day, or frequently drink its tea to help protect your eyes.

MAGICAL SWEET BREW

Fennel tea is sweet and delicious. It soothes your tummy, helping your digestion and easing belly cramps, gas and spasms.

To make fennel tea, lightly simmer 2 teaspoons of seeds in 1 cup of water, covered, for 5 minutes. Turn off the heat and let sit 10 minutes. Strain, add honey if desired, and drink.

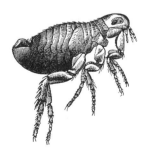

DID YOU KNOW . .
In medieval times the fennel plant, along with St. John's wort and rosemary, were hung over the door on Midsummer's Eve (June 23) to ward off evil spirits.

FLEA BOMB

Believe it or not, fennel wards off fleas! Rub powdered fennel into the coats of your dogs and cats and sprinkle it on their beds to keep the fleas away.

FENNEL FOOD

Fennel has been used as a food for thousands of years throughout the world. The seeds, leaves and root are eaten in different countries in these ways:

∾ **India:** The seeds are mixed with sugar and eaten after dinner to help digestion.

∾ **Italy & France:** The stalks and leaves are eaten raw in salads like celery.

∾ **Italy:** The chopped stalks are cooked like a green (a potherb).

∾ **China:** The seeds are used as medicine to relieve abdominal pain, indigestion, vomiting, gas, intestinal spasms due to coldness and poor appetite.

∾ **The countries surrounding the Mediterranean Sea:** Fennel is often cooked with fish. In this way it aids digestion, especially the digestion of oils.

∾ **Other:** The seeds may be cooked in other dishes, and are tasty added raw to salads.

FENNEL "CELERY" STALKS

Fennel stalks look just like celery! They are juicy as well, but have a surprising sweetness. Try some!

❀ For this you need fresh fennel. Either pick it out of the garden or buy it in the produce section of the grocery store.

❀ Cut off the bottom of the stalk root.

❀ Separate the stalks and wash.

❀ Eat as is, or cut off the green leafy part (although that part is good, too!).

PLANT ME!

Fennel is easy to grow as it thrives anywhere. Plant fennel seeds in April and watch them grow. They like plenty of sun and do well in a wet or dry place.

. . . .

FENNEL CANDY

In India fennel seeds are lightly roasted and then mixed with sugar to make a digestive aid. After dinner, people in India regularly eat a spoonful of this "fennel candy" as it eases digestion and tastes wonderful.

§ In a pan mix together 1 tablespoon fennel seeds, 1 teaspoon sugar and 1/4 teaspoon water. Heat gently on the stove until the sugar dissolves and coats the seeds.

§ Pour into a bowl. Add 2 more teaspoons fennel seeds and 2 teaspoons sugar. Mix together well and let cool.

§ Eat and enjoy!

FENNEL TOOTHPOWDER

Toothpowder cleans the teeth like toothpaste. It is just as effective, and you can vary the flavor depending on the herbs you use.

To use a toothpowder, wet your toothbrush, then pour a little toothpowder onto your palm. Press the wet toothbrush into the powder and brush your teeth.

Method one:

☺ Powder 1 tablespoon roasted fennel seeds in a nut and seed or coffee grinder, blender or food processor. Be sure to grind it into a very fine powder. If it is too coarse, it could pit the teeth over time.

☺ Pour the powder into a fine sieve or tea strainer. Gently sift the powder into a bowl. Toss out any coarse grains.

☺ Mix the sifted powder with 1 teaspoon baking soda.

☺ Store in a tin or glass jar, tightly covered. It keeps about six months.

Method two:

Add a few drops of essential oil of fennel to some baking soda. Mix to form a paste. You can purchase the essential oil at herb or health food stores.

Other herbs to use: Cinnamon whitens teeth, echinacea (coneflower) fights infections, and licorice gives a sweet flavor.

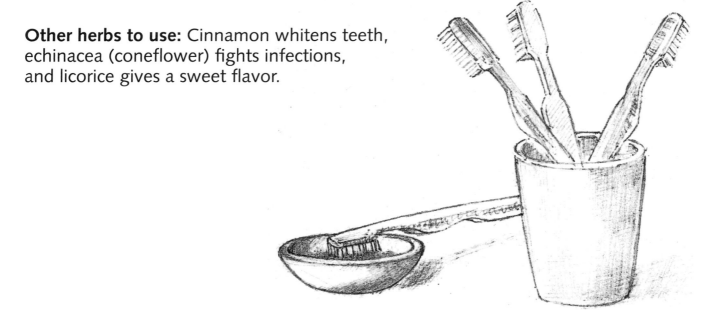

BEAN BAG BLAST

Make your own herbal bean bags! When herbs are added to bean bags, they give a delightful aroma. As you toss them back and forth or juggle with them they will scent the air and your hands.

- Cut a piece of cotton fabric 7"x 7" square.

- Fold in half, wrong side out.

- Stitch along 3 edges using very small stitches.

- Turn inside out and fill half full with beans. Kidney beans, lentils or split peas work well for this.

- Pour in 2 tablespoons of your chosen herbal mixture. Use whole or cut herbs, but not powders as they'll spill out!

- Turn under edges of open end and sew closed using very small stitches.

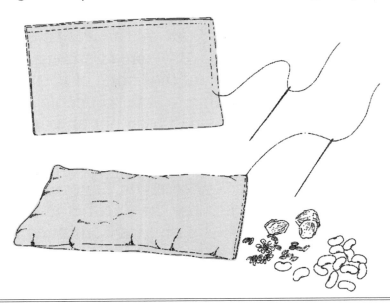

Possible Herbal Mixtures:
Sweet: fennel, licorice, anise, vanilla bean
Spicy: cinnamon, cloves, cardamom, ginger
Flowery: lavender, jasmine, geranium, rose, lavender
Relaxing: chamomile, fennel, lavender
Other: thyme, basil, eucalyptus, lemon balm

STORY TIME!
The Birth of Fennel

ong ago there lived many different tribes of people on the shores of a large warm sea. Each tribe had its own special customs and skills. Yet, rather than respect and enjoy each other's unusual gifts, the tribes only noticed their differences. Each tribe ate different foods, ruled their people differently and worshipped in different ways. Each tribe thought they had the one and only right way to do these things, and so they were constantly at war with one another.

One day a plague spread throughout the land, affecting all the tribes. Every child fell ill with stomach cramps and severe pain. The children couldn't eat and cried day and night. The tribal healers tried to cure the children with their various medicines, yet nothing worked. Soon all the wars stopped as parents tried to comfort and heal their children. Word spread among the tribes that all their children shared the same disease and that none of their cures worked.

An idea then occurred at the same time to several people in many of the tribes. They thought that if all the tribes met together and asked the Creator for help at the same moment, a cure would then appear. This idea was passed among the tribes around the sea and a day was chosen to do this.

On the appointed day, all the tribes gathered on their respective shores of the sea. Each tribe in its own way asked the Creator that all children be made well again, regardless of their tribe. This gathering continued for a long time. Suddenly a mist arose over the water. It increased in size until it engulfed the entire shoreline surrounding the sea.

Wonder spread rapidly throughout the people when they saw it. The mist swirled and thickened, spreading inland several miles. Soon everyone was in a dense fog, one so thick no one could see beyond his or her own hands. The fog quieted the children, as if it was healing them. Then as quickly as it had come, the misty fog thinned and disappeared.

People looked at each other in amazement. All about them stood tall green plants they had never seen before. The plants had thick juicy stalks ending in long tapers surrounded by feathery green leaves. Large flower heads stood out, filled by dozens of tiny yellow-green seeds. They just knew this plant was sent to heal their children and they all fell to their knees in thanksgiving. The children thought it was so delicious, they ate every part of the plant—stalk, leaves and seeds. Soon the children were well again, laughing and playing as before.

The adults ate the plant, too, and began cooking with it. Of course every tribe created different recipes, but this time they shared their ideas and creations with each other. The new healing plant became a common link among all people. Soon the tribes began to trade and agree with each other rather than fight.

We still use this delicious herb today. Called fennel, it is widely eaten in many countries, just as it was in the past. Children especially love its sweet taste when they chew its stalks, leaves and seeds.

MULLEIN
The Ear and Lung Herb

Mullein is an unusual-looking herb. It has broad, fuzzy leaves. When flowering it shoots up a very tall stem. Bees love the tiny yellow flowers. You will, too, as they make a wonderful healing oil for earaches.

USE MULLEIN FOR:

* earaches and inflammations
* coughs, especially dry cough and whooping cough
* colds, flu, mumps
* bronchitis, asthma
* bleeding
* skin problems—eczema, bruises, frostbite
* hemorrhoids
* diarrhea
* nerve pain

Latin Name: *Verbascum thapsus*
Parts Used: leaves and flowers
Energy and Taste: neutral energy; mildly pleasant taste
Dose for Children: Drink 1/4-1/2 cup of tea 3-4 times daily. Sweeten with honey, if desired. For earaches, put 2-5 drops mullein oil in the ear every 3-4 hours until the earache is gone.
Make as a: tea, oil, poultice, salve, tincture, gargle, salve, wash, syrup, pill, powder, capsule, fomentation, ear drops.

Mullein Plant

yellow

silvery green

green

TOUCH AND FEEL

Find a mullein plant and run your hands along its leaves. Do they feel rough? soft? Do they remind you of any animals?

Touch the tall stalk. What does it feel like? What could you use the stalk for?

Now gently stroke a mullein flower. How do the flowers feel? Smell the leaves, the stalk, the flowers. What do they smell like to you?

BREATHE-FREELY HEALING POTION

Mullein leaves and root are excellent for bronchitis, tonsillitis, pleurisy, pneumonia and coughs, including whooping cough. It especially heals clear yellow to green mucus from the lungs and throat.

For best results, make a decoction tea of 1 teaspoon mullein leaves and root, 1 teaspoon elder, 1 teaspoon wild cherry bark and ½ teaspoon licorice root to 1½ cups of water.

MULLEIN CANDLES

Hundreds of years ago people would dip dry mullein stalks into fat and then light them for torches, like huge candles. Mullein stalks worked well for this because they are so thick and tall.

Can you imagine a long procession of mullein torches on a dark night? If you try making a torch, be sure to wear gloves so the suet doesn't drip onto your hands.

Draw a picture of mullein torches at night.

MULLEIN SWORDS

Children in the past used the long stalks of mullein for sword fights. After you pick all the flowers to make mullein oil, break two stalks above the leaves near their base. Then use the stalks as swords with a friend.

HERBAL OILS

Herbal oils are made by extracting the medicine of herbs into an oil. They are used on the outside of the body. Herbal oils are valuable for sore and aching muscles, painful joints, cuts, bites, stings, wounds, bruises, eczema, skin irritations, burns, headaches and earaches. They can be rubbed on the chest or back for colds, flu and lung congestion.

The specific use of an oil is determined by the herbs used. Oils keep up to a year. Store in glass bottles in a cool dark place.

To make:

❧ Rub your chosen herbs (fresh or dried) between the palms of your hands to break the herbs down and release their juices (called "bruising" the herbs).

❧ Place the herbs in a glass jar.

❧ Pour olive or sesame oil over the herbs until there is 1 inch of oil standing above the herbs.

❧ Cover the jar tightly with a lid and set in a dark cool place away from sunlight.

❧ Shake the jar for one minute every day for the next two weeks so the herbs and oil mix well. If you are using fresh herbs, only leave them in the oil for 2-3 days before pressing the oil out. The water in the fresh herbs will hasten rancidity, so oils made with fresh herbs may not keep as long as those made with dry herbs.

❧ Strain the oil by covering a kitchen colander with cheesecloth or an old dishtowel. Set the colander in a large bowl. Pour the herbal oil into the colander. The herbs collect in the cloth while the oil runs through into the bowl. Squeeze the herbs in the cloth to extract the remaining oil. Throw away the herbs and keep the oil.

❧ Add 400 IU vitamin E to 1 cup of oil as a preservative.

❧ Pour the oil into a glass jar and cover tightly.

❧ Store in a cool, dark place.

TIME FOR A MASSAGE!

A Swedish massage rubs oil all over the skin, easing sore muscles, aches and pains. It is also one of the best ways to relax, as it feels great!

Herbal oils make good massage oils. Different herbs, such as chamomile, elder, lavender and roses, help relax the muscles. Others good for the skin are chamomile, calendula, elder, slippery elm, plantain, yarrow, comfrey or mullein. Some herbs added to scent the oil are lavender, nutmeg, cloves, rosemary, rose petals, lemon balm and even vanilla. This makes your skin smell wonderful! A few drops of an essential oil can also be added.

Make an herbal massage oil and trade foot rubs with a friend.

VAPOR RUB

Make your own vapor rub to relieve lung congestion and coughs. Mix together in a glass bottle:

* 1/2 cup mullein oil (or olive oil)

* 1/4 teaspoon eucalyptus essential oil

* 1/8 teaspoon each lemon balm and thyme essential oils

* Shake well and massage onto your throat, chest or back.

* Cover with a warm washcloth or piece of flannel.

MULLEIN OIL

Make an herbal oil using mullein flowers and olive oil. This is a useful remedy for many things: earaches, inflammations of the inner ear, discharges from the ear, eczema, bruises and frostbite. It also works extremely well for almost all earaches when combined with the herbs St. John's wort and garlic.

HERBAL EAR DROPS

ar oils relieve pain and inflammation in the ear. They are made with herbs that are antibiotic and fight infections. Herbal ear drops keep about a year. Store in a glass bottle in a cool dark place.

- Make or purchase herbal ear drops.
- Have the person lie on his/her side with the affected ear up.
- Drip 2-5 drops into the affected ear.
- Place a small cotton ball into the ear to prevent the oil from spilling out.
- Have the person continue lying on his/her side for 5-10 minutes more. Keep the cotton ball in place.
- Repeat this process 5-6 times throughout the day until the symptoms are gone.
- A hot water bottle on the ear often speeds the healing process. In fact, earaches can often be relieved by heat alone if you immediately place a hot water bottle against the affected ear. Leave in place as long as it feels good. (If it doesn't feel good, do not use the hot water bottle.)

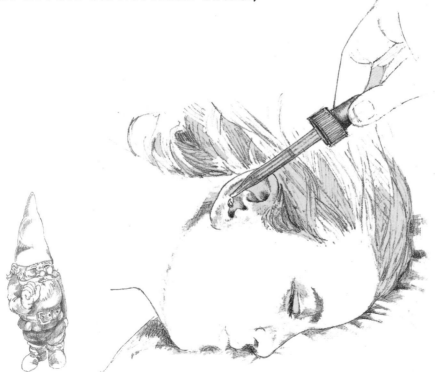

Herbs to use: mullein, echinacea (coneflower), calendula, garlic.

NOTE: Do not use if the eardrum is ruptured.

STORY TIME!
The Young Rabbit

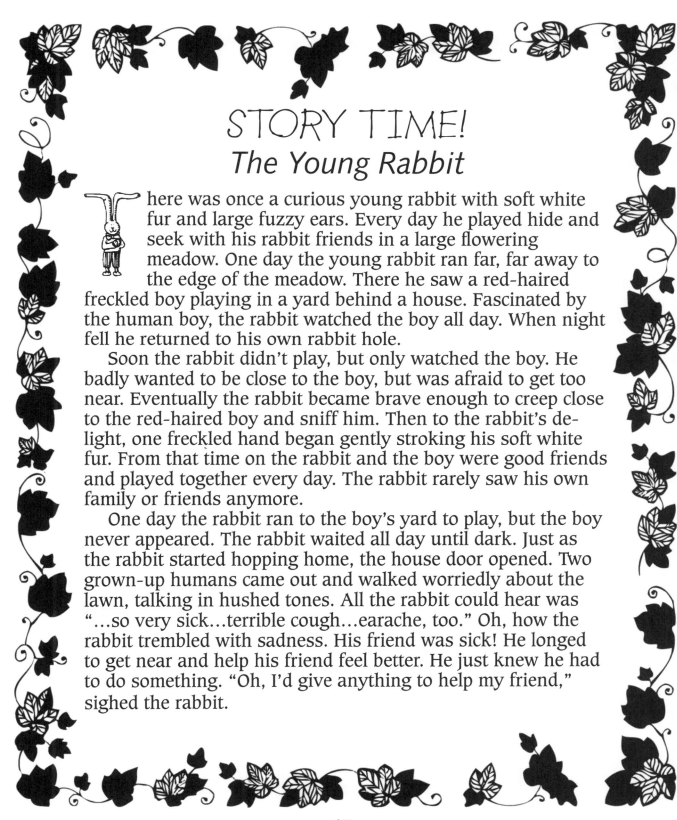

There was once a curious young rabbit with soft white fur and large fuzzy ears. Every day he played hide and seek with his rabbit friends in a large flowering meadow. One day the young rabbit ran far, far away to the edge of the meadow. There he saw a red-haired freckled boy playing in a yard behind a house. Fascinated by the human boy, the rabbit watched the boy all day. When night fell he returned to his own rabbit hole.

Soon the rabbit didn't play, but only watched the boy. He badly wanted to be close to the boy, but was afraid to get too near. Eventually the rabbit became brave enough to creep close to the red-haired boy and sniff him. Then to the rabbit's delight, one freckled hand began gently stroking his soft white fur. From that time on the rabbit and the boy were good friends and played together every day. The rabbit rarely saw his own family or friends anymore.

One day the rabbit ran to the boy's yard to play, but the boy never appeared. The rabbit waited all day until dark. Just as the rabbit started hopping home, the house door opened. Two grown-up humans came out and walked worriedly about the lawn, talking in hushed tones. All the rabbit could hear was "…so very sick…terrible cough…earache, too." Oh, how the rabbit trembled with sadness. His friend was sick! He longed to get near and help his friend feel better. He just knew he had to do something. "Oh, I'd give anything to help my friend," sighed the rabbit.

Suddenly, a queer six inch tall man with a lumpy green hat and red pointed shoes appeared. He walked slowly toward the rabbit, his gnarled hands leaning on a carved wooden staff. "*Anything?*" the odd man asked.

Startled, the rabbit gulped, "Who are you?"

The strange man peered at the rabbit. "My name is Mr. Greenleaf. I am the herbal magician of these parts. You were wishing to help your friend, and I ask again, would you give anything to help him?"

The rabbit answered quickly, "Yes, oh yes, anything!"

"Even your life as a rabbit?" Mr. Greenleaf asked.

The rabbit hesitated thoughtfully but finally answered. "I love my friend and I would be willing to give my life to save him."

Mr. Greenleaf looked at the rabbit queerly for a long time. Then reaching into a brown bag he had flung over one shoulder, he took out a thick root and set it in front of the rabbit. "This root is magical," he said mysteriously. "If you want to save your friend, then you must eat it before the moon is directly overhead. After that, it will lose its magic. However, when you eat the root, you will not be a rabbit anymore." Then Mr. Greenleaf vanished.

The young rabbit didn't stir. He thought long and hard about what the strange man had said. As the moon slowly rose in the dark night sky, he thought of his rabbit family and friends. He remembered playing hide and seek through the rabbit tunnels, eating warm green grass and dozing in the afternoon sun. As he recalled how wonderful it felt to snuggle into his own burrow, its warmth beckoned to him. He hadn't seen his family lately and he missed them terribly. "No, I won't eat the root," the rabbit thought. "I love my family and friends too much." He roughly pushed the root away with his paw.

The moon was nearly overhead when the rabbit looked one last time at his friend's house. Suddenly the boy's silhouette appeared in a window. Fond memories of what they had shared flooded over him—food from the garden, games in the yard, the boy's gentle touches. Love filled the rabbit's heart and he realized that his love for the young boy was even greater than his love for his snug rabbit home. Without hesitating the rabbit reached for the root and ate it.

Before one could say "mullein root," the rabbit changed into a plant. Its white root reached deep into the earth and then sprouted a thick stalk with soft, large leaves like rabbit ears. The thick white root and the fuzzy leaves were all that remained to remind us that the plant had once been a white furry rabbit with big floppy ears.

When the sun rose, Mr. Greenleaf appeared. "You have made one of the greatest wishes of all, my friend," he said, "and now you will be blessed for it." Mr. Greenleaf mumbled some magic words and instantly grew to human size. Then he gently picked several leaves and yellow flowers off the rabbit-plant. Taking these to the boy's mother, he showed her how to make a medicinal tea and oil from the plant. They would heal the boy's lungs and ears.

Some say that plants don't have feelings. Those who know the secret life of plants, however, are able to see the happiness and joy of the plant-that-once-was-a-rabbit, a rabbit who transformed his life into a healing herb so his childhood friend might live.

Mr. Greenleaf came to all the rabbits and other magic meadow creatures. He told everyone what had happened, and then announced, "This special plant is now called mullein. It is destined to grow proud and tall all over the world. It will help many people, especially children, just as the rabbit helped his friend."

Now this is how the mullein plant came to be. You, too, can feel the softness of the mullein's leaves and remember the story about the young rabbit's gift of love.

Mullein Song

Michael Tierra

GARLIC
The Cold and Flu Spice

 arlic is said to cure every ailment but the one it causes: garlic breath! The ancient Egyptians and Greeks used it for many illnesses, and today it is still a powerful and useful healing herb. Garlic is most effective when it is fresh or juiced. Garlic that is cooked or has its odor removed tastes good, but is no longer a strong medicine for the body

USE GARLIC FOR:

* colds, flu
* fever
* coughs
* pneumonia, bronchitis, asthma and other lung disorders
* hoarseness, sore throat
* difficulty breathing
* parasites, worms
* wounds, sores, lumps
* earaches
* weak digestion
* poor circulation
* joint pains
* cramps, spasms

Latin Name: *Allium sativum*
Part Used: bulb
Energy and Taste: hot energy; spicy taste
Dose for Children: 1/2 teaspoon every hour of the syrup, oil or juice; 1/3-1 raw clove once or twice a day.
Make as a: spice, food, syrup, plaster, oil, tincture, ear drops, paste, salve, tea, dried bouquet, juice.

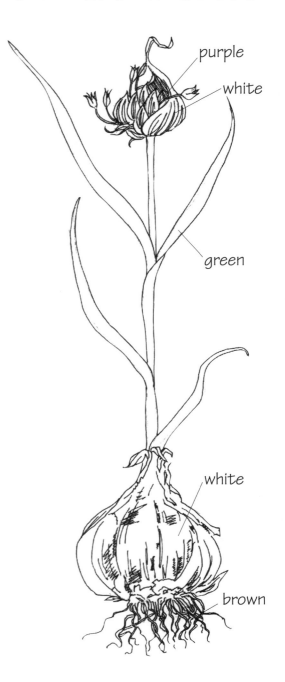

Garlic Plant

purple

white

green

white

brown

PHEW! GARLIC!

When garlic is rubbed on the feet, its odor can be smelled on the breath within seconds! That's how quickly and effectively garlic can move through the body.

If you are concerned about the odor of garlic on your breath, eat a few sprigs of parsley. Parsley helps neutralize garlic odor.

GARLIC JUICE

Garlic juice is one of the very best remedies for lung complaints such as coughs, colds, bronchitis, pneumonia, lung congestion and mucus. Take 1/2 tsp. every hour, or as needed. Store in a jar in the refrigerator.

∾ Press or mash 1 or more bulbs of garlic into enough apple cider vinegar or olive oil to cover and mix well.

∾ Allow to stand for a day or two.

∾ Place this in cheesecloth or a thin cotton towel.

∾ Wring and squeeze repeatedly, collecting the juice in a cup.

Note: Pure garlic juice can sometimes be purchased in grocery stores. It is usually found in the spice section. It tastes great added to soups, vegetables and salad dressings!

SNAPPY CIDER

This vinegar tincture is good for sinus infections, colds, flu, mucus congestion and lung complaints. Take 1/2-1 teaspoon every hour. It can keep for 2 years. Store in a glass bottle in a cool dark place.

- Use equal parts of the following: minced onion and garlic, grated fresh ginger and horseradish, mustard seeds and black peppercorns.

- Mince or grate the fresh herbs.

- Combine the seeds and peppercorns.

- Add 1 or more whole cayenne chilies (depending on how spicy you want it!).

- Mix all together in a glass jar.

- Pour vinegar into the bottle, leaving a 1" layer of liquid over the herbs. Shake the bottle daily to mix the herbs and liquid. Leave for 2 weeks.

- Strain: place a cotton cloth in a colander and set in a big bowl. Pour in vinegar mixture. Squeeze the herbs to extract the remaining liquid. Strain a second time.

- Add 1 part honey or glycerin to 3 parts of the vinegar tincture to preserve it.

- Bottle by pouring into a clean bottle. Label and date.

PLASTERS

 A plaster is an herbal mash that is wrapped in a cloth or combined with a thick oil and then placed directly on the skin. It is placed in the cloth or oil to prevent the strong herbs (such as garlic or ground mustard seeds) from burning the skin.

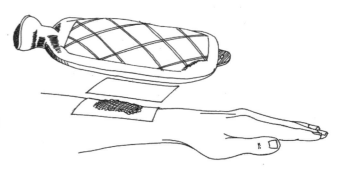

* Powder or mash desired herbs in a nut and seed grinder, blender or food processor.

* Mix with olive oil to form a thick paste.

* Spread paste on a piece of cheesecloth or thin towel. Wrap up until the paste is enclosed in the cloth.

* Place on the skin where desired.

* Keep warm with a hot water bottle or heating pad.

* Change frequently if needed.

* It can burn delicate skin, so if the skin looks red and feels too hot, the plaster's job is done and it should be removed.

DO THE GARLIC MASH!

A garlic plaster is excellent for stopping severe coughs and colds:

• Mince several cloves of garlic.

• Mix with olive oil to form a mash.

• Wrap this in cotton or cheesecloth and tape to the soles of your feet for an hour, or even overnight. (Some people with delicate skin can experience irritation, so check how this feels on you before you leave it on too long.)

Garlic is quickly absorbed through the skin in this way and moves through the body to treat the lungs. A garlic plaster can also be placed directly over the chest.

GARLIC "SANDWICHES"?

You can find garlic in almost all kitchens as it makes food taste delicious. Here is one recipe that is a traditional Italian appetizer. Not only is it delicious, but it helps heal coughs and lung congestion with white mucus, as well as bronchitis, pneumonia, asthma, colds and flu!

* Press all cloves of garlic in one garlic bulb.

* Pour enough olive oil over the garlic to make it slightly thick, but not runny.

* Dip pieces of bread into the mixture, thickly coating them with the garlic.

* Eat and enjoy!

YUCK! WORMS!

Worms in the garden are our friends, but worms in our body cause illness. Garlic chases those worms and other parasites out of the body. But you have to eat a lot of garlic for it to work!

First thing, stop feeding worms "worm food," which is sugar! Then, eat 2-4 raw cloves of garlic every day until the worms are gone. Perhaps the best way to eat garlic is in a garlic "sandwich." You can also take 1/2 teaspoon of garlic oil 2-4 times a day.

ENCHANTED GARLIC SYRUP

This syrup is especially good for stubborn coughs, bronchitis, pneumonia, mucus and lung congestion due to coldness (when there is clear to white mucus). If there is heat (high fever, slight chills, and yellow mucus), then eliminate the ginger and cayenne. Take in teaspoon doses every two hours or as needed.

Mix together thoroughly:

- 1/2 cup lemon juice (freshly squeezed is preferable)
- 1/2 cup water
- 5 large cloves garlic, minced or pressed
- 1 teaspoon grated fresh ginger or 1/4 teaspoon ginger powder
- a dash of cayenne powder
- 1/2 cup honey

STORY TIME!
The Evil Phantom

Long ago an evil phantom stalked the earth and attacked people, making them ill. It did this by flying through the back of their necks and into their bodies. Then it would create a terrible sickness inside. Headaches, sore throats, fevers, chills, body aches, coughs, all overcame the poor victims. For days and nights the sick lay thrashing in bed, not able to eat or even stand up. Sometimes the evil phantom leapt off one person and attacked another. Often the entire family came down with this terrible sickness.

People covered their necks to prevent the phantom from attacking them. Although this made it more difficult for the ghoul, if people ever uncovered their necks, it quickly pounced on them and worked its ugly ways. Then its evil laughter cackled through the air and chilled people to the bone.

One day a young boy was playing happily when he saw the dark phantom flying through the misty sky. It was an ugly and hideous sight. Drool slobbered out of its open mouth, and it was coated with a sickly-looking mottled green and black slime. Its claw-like hands pinched open and shut, as if demanding to snatch up another victim. The boy shuddered when he saw it flying overhead and heard its teeth and bones clacking. Terrified, he screamed in horror.

The phantom instantly charged at the boy, teasing and taunting him, like a cat playing with a mouse. The boy ran blindly into a building, desperately trying to evade the evil creature. But the ghoul flew through the walls in close pursuit. Next, the boy ran out of the village and into the woods. Dodging behind the trees he threw sticks

and rocks at the monstrous phantom. Yet the ghoul could easily pass through everything. It seemed truly indestructible.

The phantom clutched at the boy. Then with a great screeching cry, it lunged at his neck. Swerving, the boy threw himself down a steep hill. Rolling down the slippery slope, the boy tumbled onto the meadow beyond. There he grasped the first thing his hand found and flung it at the hideous monster.

Suddenly, the ghoul shrieked in disgust and backed away. The boy saw that what he had thrown was the common garlic plant his family used to flavor food. The phantom took advantage of the boy's distraction and charged at his neck again. Clinging tightly, the ghoul started to enter the boy's body.

In one last desperate attempt, the boy pulled up another plant, bit into the garlic bulb and ate several cloves. Immediately the potent herb spread throughout his body. Shrieking with rage and horror, the monster slithered down the boy's back and onto the ground. Then slowly, right before the boy's eyes, it disintegrated into a wailing and moaning sticky green and black mass. Soon it disappeared altogether and was seldom seen again. Garlic had saved the boy. From that day on people ate garlic when they felt the ghoul might be around trying to make them sick.

GARLIC THOSE GERMS AWAY!

If you want to prevent getting sick with a cold, flu or lung ailment, then do the following: Wrap a clove of crushed garlic in a piece of cloth and pin to your undershirt. Change every other day. The garlic odor kills germs in the air and keeps them from causing illness. This is an old folk remedy that really works! You can also eat a little fresh garlic every day. Add it to salad dressings, pasta and soups right before they are served.

GARLIC EAR OIL

Like mullein, garlic oil is good for earaches. It especially eases those that feel better with heat, such as a hot water bottle. When you are ready to use it, heat a teaspoonful of the oil (over a candle flame works well). When it is warm, place 2-3 drops in the ear every 2-3 hours.

∾ Mince one large bulb of garlic.

∾ Place in a double boiler and cover garlic with enough olive oil to form a 1" layer on top.

∾ Heat slowly and gently for one hour.

∾ Cool, strain and refrigerate.

NOTE: Do not use garlic oil for swimmers' ear (use echinacea tincture instead), or if you suspect a punctured eardrum.

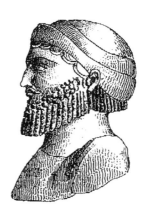

BELIEVE IT OR NOT!

It's true! Ulysses in the Odyssey used garlic to escape his companions' fate—being changed into a pig by Circe!

PLANTAIN
The Bee Sting Plant

Plantain is a familiar herb found all over the United States—in vacant lots, by roadsides, in meadowlands, between sidewalk cracks, even in your own yard! Although it is usually called a weed, it is wise to let this important herb grow because of its many valuable uses.

The Native Americans used plantain seeds as food. They called it "Whiteman's foot" because it was brought over by early European settlers. The seeds stuck to their feet and then scattered wherever they walked throughout the land.

PLANTAIN IS USED FOR:
* infections
* inflammations
* bee stings
* snakebites
* cuts, wounds, sores
* skin infections
* poison oak & ivy
* swellings

Latin Name: *Plantago major* (wide-leaf plantain); *Plantago lanceolata* (lance-leaf plantain)

Parts Used: leaves, seeds and root

Energy and Taste: cool energy; pleasant, mildly bitter taste

Dose for Children: Drink 1/4-1/2 cup every 2 hours. Sweeten as needed. As the symptoms lessen, gradually decrease the amount to 1/4-1/2 cup 2-3 times a day for 3 days or until all the symptoms are gone.

Make as a: tea, poultice, pill, salve, syrup, wash, capsule, fomentation, powder, eyewash, foot powder, oil, baby powder, lip balm.

Plantain Plant

yellow-brown

green

POULTICES

A poultice is made when an herb is mashed and placed directly on the skin. It can be left in place several hours and overnight. A poultice should be changed several times a day for 2-3 days to be effective.

A quick poultice is made by picking the herb (make sure it has not been sprayed with chemicals), washing it, then chewing it up. Don't swallow this, but spit out the herbal mash and put that directly on the wound. There are a lot of healing organisms in saliva. (That's why dogs and cats lick their wounds to heal them!) You can also steam the fresh or dry herb for several minutes, then mash it up and put it on the skin. Or mix plantain powder with water and tape this paste on the skin.

Another method is to steam the leaves lightly in a little water or blend them in a food processor to form a mash. Then mash them together and place on a piece of clean cotton or cheesecloth. Tape the cloth (with mash inside) on the skin over the desired area.

The plantain mash can be stored for future use by pouring it into an ice cube tray and freezing it. Keep the frozen cubes in a plastic bag. Then when you need a poultice, melt a cube in a pan on the stove!

MAGICAL HERBAL WASHES

Herbal washes are used to treat skin conditions such as poison oak or ivy, measles or other skin eruptions. They are also an especially helpful method for giving herbs to infants. The skin absorbs the tea and the herb then treats the body. To prepare:

◆ Make a tea of your chosen herb(s).

◆ Dip a washcloth into the tea and wash the desired area with it.

◆ Let the tea air-dry on the skin.

◆ Repeat several times a day as needed.

YIKES! POISON OAK AND IVY!

Plantain is often very effective in treating poison oak or ivy. Make an herbal wash of the plantain leaves. Wash the itchy area 5-6 times a day for 2-3 days to make the red rash go away. (A plantain poultice also works well.) It is even better if you drink plantain tea 3 times daily as well.

FEEL BETTER FAST BREW

Plantain tea reduces swellings in the body and helps to heal bladder and kidney infections. You can also use the tea as a wash for rashes, bites or poison oak and ivy.

* Stuff a small pot full of fresh plantain leaves, or use 1 heaping teaspoon dried leaves per cup of water.

* Pour boiling water over the plantain and cover.

* Let sit 15-20 minutes.

* Cool, strain and drink, or use as a wash.

FAIRY BANDAGE

Plantain is often called "nature's bandage," or a fairy bandage, because it can stick to the skin all by itself. In this way it not only draws out bee stingers, but splinters, too. Use a plantain poultice for this and change it frequently. (Plantain once pulled several pieces of metal out of a person's hand within three days, preventing the need for surgery.)

Plantain also heals wounds, scrapes, cuts and burns. Its soothing effect is felt within minutes after applying it to the skin.

PLANTAIN WINDOW PICTURE

Here is a fun way to frame plantain in a window so you can see the fascinating veins in its leaves better. Pick a few plantain leaves, wash and dry carefully on a towel. Cut two pieces of waxed paper larger than the plantain leaves. Lay one sheet of waxed paper down and place the plantain leaves on it in any shape or design you choose. Then lay the second sheet of waxed paper on top of the plantain leaves.

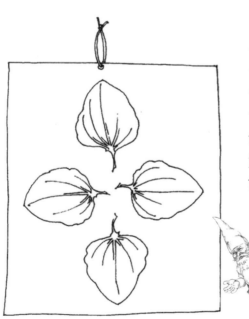

Now, put a towel over this plantain "sandwich" and lightly iron it until the two sheets of waxed paper stick together. Next, trim the edges of the waxed paper. Punch a hole in the top of the paper and thread a string through it. Hang the plantain picture in a window where light can shine through it!

RUB DOWN!

The long ribbed leaves of plantain make it a very good plant for a leaf print rubbing. You can also use other plant leaves as you like. Choose a variety and do several on one page.

Rubbings work best with thin paper. You can use tracing paper, thin typing paper, even onionskin paper. You'll also need soft colored pencils, crayons or chalk. Use one color or choose several for one rubbing.

- ✎ Place your chosen leaves on a hard surface.

- ✎ Cover them with a thin sheet of paper. Hold the paper securely in place.

- ✎ Using light pressure, make back-and-forth strokes over the leaves with the pencils, crayons or chalk, until the leaf images appear on the paper.

- ✎ Hang your leaf print rubbing for all to see and enjoy. Or make note paper by folding the paper in half with the print on the outside.

DID YOU KNOW . . .

☞ Plantain was once called ribwort because of its long, striking veins.

☞ In an old country game, children would hit the flower-stalk heads against each other until one of the stalks broke. The winner held the un-broken stalk

STING EASE

When plantain is put directly on a bee sting, it very quickly stops the pain. The best way to use plantain for bee stings is as a poultice. But you can also saturate a cotton ball in plantain tea and tape it over the sting. Usually doing this once is enough, but repeat as needed.

Plantain Song

Michael Tierra

Dm   C   B♭   Am   Gm

Plan tain, plan - tain, I call you plan - tain, you grow e - very -

Am   Dm   AM   Gm   B♭

where that I'm plan - ting. Some call you a weed with the po - wer to

Dm   Am   Dm   Am   Dm

cure bites and stings, and to cure u - ri - na - ry in - fections. Plan -

Dm   C   Am   Dm

tain, plan - tain, sim - ple herb called plan - tain.

STORY TIME!

How Fluffy Cloud Gave Plantain Herb to the Earth

nce there was a fluffy cloud that lived high in the sky. Every so often the cloud would grow dark as it filled with water from the earth and then uncontrollably showered rain upon all the plants and creatures below. When it was the sun's turn to shine, Fluffy Cloud would thin into tiny wisps and let the sunlight down from the sky. In this way the sun and clouds played catch with the rains of heaven. In the process of having such fun, they also gave the important water that is necessary for all plants, insects and creatures living on earth to grow.

Now our cloud could have lived happily ever after just like all the other clouds in the sky, except that one day it realized it could not be fully happy so long as someone below was unhappy. This usually happened whenever it released its storage of rain when everyone below was unprepared for it.

Fluffy Cloud was silly to wish that it could rain only when everyone was ready for it. This was impossible, because everyone knows that people never agree to be happy at the same time. For a well-wishing puff of mist such as Fluffy Cloud it was a special problem, since who is happy when it rains during a picnic, ballgame, parade or outdoor birthday party?

Unable to realize any of this, Fluffy Cloud was left with no choice but to feel increasingly unhappy whenever it had to release its showers. No matter what, there was always someone who didn't want it to rain—not just then, anyway. The problem became worse, since whenever Fluffy Cloud tried to hold back its rain for several days or weeks, eventually it would burst. Then too much rain came down all at once. This caused real disasters and unhappiness as rivers flooded their banks and sometimes even soaked people's basements.

One day as Fluffy Cloud thought long and hard about this problem, it heard a rumor going around the heavens. The news spread from star to star, moon to earth, planets to comets and comets to asteroids, until at last (as usual), the clouds heard about it. The rumor claimed that a rare and special event was about to occur: soon both the sun and the moon would actually shine together at the same time.

Now such an auspicious event always meant an opportunity for rare magic to occur. When our little cloud realized this, it suddenly had a brilliant idea. Fluffy Cloud would use the magic to give a special gift to people in exchange for the good times they missed when it had to rain. Quickly, the little cloud told the sun and the moon about its plan and asked for their help.

When the eventful day arrived, Fluffy Cloud took a special position in the sky so that it could cover a large area. Then, when the exact moment came, the sun and moon carefully beamed all their rays into the cloud, filling it with light instead of the usual water. When it was so stuffed it could hold no more light, the magic happened.

Fluffy Cloud burst open and showered down special cloud-light seeds instead of water. Wherever the light seeds touched the ground, a small green plant sprouted up. It had ribs like the rays of the sun and moon. A long stem held a crown of tiny white flowers that seemed to reflect the light back to the skies. This was indeed a magical plant, for it had many healing properties.

Now these plants began to spring up everywhere: in meadows, at the edges of forests, in flower and vegetable gardens, even in patches of dirt along roads and sidewalks. In time, so many plants came up in spots where they weren't wanted that many people forgot they were Fluffy Cloud's special gift. People began to treat them like weeds. They wouldn't eat the plants because they didn't taste good enough for that. And they wouldn't pick their flowers because they were much too small and hardly as attractive as a nearby rose bush or peony.

Eventually these people began to curse these plants and poison or yank them out of the ground. All the while they muttered to themselves over and over, "Why must you grow everywhere I'm planting ... everywhere I'm planting ... planting, planting, planting?" Faster and faster they said those words until soon the mysterious plant was called "plantain." (To see how this might happen, try saying "planting, planting, planting" as fast as you can and you'll see how it changes into "plantain.")

When Fluffy Cloud saw this, it realized that raining magic seeds didn't change people's happiness. It learned that some people choose to be happy and receptive no matter what happens, while others become closed, unhappy and resistant even when given a special gift. Fluffy Cloud was sad until it saw that some people did appreciate its magic gift after all.

These folks learned about plantain's tremendous healing powers. Plantain could relieve the pain of injuries, burns, bites and stings, purify the blood, clear the waters of the body, relieve fever and even draw out slivers.

Now those who prefer a happy ending to this story choose to remember the special healing gifts of plantain. They lovingly thank Fluffy Cloud and its impossible attempt to make everyone happy. And they are grateful that no matter where they step, plantain now grows everywhere.

CHAMOMILE
The Calm Child Herb

The tiny golden flowers of chamomile are so beautiful, they look like smiling little suns. Chamomile grows all over the United States and Europe. It is a popular European beverage that has been enjoyed for centuries. In fact, Alice of *Alice in Wonderland* drank chamomile tea. Peter Rabbit did, too! Chamomile has many important uses for healing our bodies, too.

Chamomile Plant

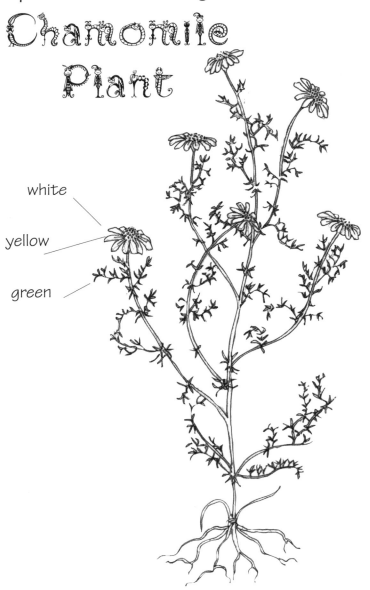

white
yellow
green

USE CHAMOMILE FOR:
* stomachache
* indigestion
* gas
* colic
* nervousness, tension
* restlessness
* crying, whining, irritability
* teething
* insomnia
* colds
* bowel problems such as constipation
* burns, cuts
* sore muscles
* diaper rash and other rashes

Latin Name: *Anthemis nobilis* or *Matricaria chamomilla*
Part Used: flowers
Energy and Taste: neutral energy; bittersweet taste
Dose for Children: Chamomile is a very mild and safe herb, although for some people too much chamomile tea can cause frequent bowel movements. (This is great if you are constipated!) Drink up to 3 cups of tea a day as desired or needed.
Make as a: tea, bath, capsule, pill, suntea, fomentation, wash, poultice, tincture, bitters, dream pillow, mouthwash, steam, oil, salve.

TOUCH AND FEEL

Lie down in a bed of chamomile flowers.
(If you can't find them, then imagine it.)
What does it smell like? How does it feel?
Look up through the dozens of tiny flowers.
Now play the Game of Imagination.

GAME OF IMAGINATION

ie down on your tummy. Look closely at the tiny chamomile flowers and their feathery leaves. Imagine yourself getting smaller and smaller until you feel yourself sitting on top of one of the flowers. How do you feel? What does the plant look like from the top of the flower?

When you are done, imagine yourself growing back to normal size. Now try drawing and coloring a picture of you sitting on top of a chamomile flower.

DID YOU KNOW . . .

☞ There are many species of chamomile. Two of the most commonly used are the bitter Roman chamomile, and the apple-sweet German chamomile. In fact, chamomile is named *manzanilla* in Latin, meaning "little apple," because of the apple-sweet taste of the German species.

☞ Chamomile has been widely used throughout Europe and the Mediterranean countries for a very long time. The ancient Egyptians respected the plant and the early Greek and Roman doctors gave chamomile for headaches. In old times the German and English herbalists used it for digestive problems and cramps. In fact, in England it is regarded as a "bandage for the stomach."

☞ In France and Spain the medical profession recognizes chamomile as a valuable children's herb for colic, upset stomach and sleeplessness.

FLOWERED WALKWAY

It may be hard to believe, but you can actually walk on chamomile flowers! Chamomile is used as a ground cover and is planted as a "green walk" in gardens. When people walk on a chamomile path a strong, fragrant scent fills the air.

Plant a chamomile walkway in your yard or garden.

TEMPER-TAMING POTION

Chamomile tea is very calming and relaxing. It soothes irritability and bad tempers. The next time you feel a teensy bit crabby, drink some chamomile tea right away and see how much better you feel! Add some licorice to make it sweet and even more effective.

* Place 2 teaspoons chamomile flowers (and 1/2 teaspoon chopped licorice, if desired) in a teapot or stainless steel pot.

* Pour 1 cup of boiling water over the flowers.

* Put a lid on and let sit for 15-20 minutes.

* Strain, sweeten to taste and drink in 1/4-1/2 cup doses.

RUB-A-DUB-DUB: LET'S TAKE AN HERBAL BATH!

An herbal bath is a fun type of bath to have. It turns the bath water different colors, and it smells good, too. Also, it is very easy to make.
Here's how:

 Fill a cotton cloth bag (muslin is good) with your chosen herbs. Use about 1$\frac{1}{2}$ cups of herbs to a bathtub full of water. (This is about an ounce of dried leaves or flowers.)

 Tie the bag shut and hang it from the bathtub faucet directly under the flow of water.

 As hot water fills the tub, it will run through the herbs and press out their essences.

 You can also place the herb bag right into the tub with you.

For a stronger herbal bath:

 Make a tea using 2 cups of herbs to 2 quarts of water.

 Bring the water to a boil, turn off the heat, add your chosen herbs, cover and let them steep for 20 minutes.

 Strain and pour the tea directly into the bath water.

Herbs to Use: *chamomile, calendula, lemon balm, ginger.*

SECRET REMEDY FOR SWEET DREAMS!

Chamomile is calming, helping you sleep better and feel more relaxed. Before bed take a chamomile bath. Next, drink a cup of chamomile tea. Then get ready for a good night's sleep. Sweet dreams! (You can also mix 1 teaspoon chamomile with 1 teaspoon lemon balm and 1/2 teaspoon fennel to 1 cup boiling water for a great tasting sleep tea.)

TUMMY-ACHE TEA

Does your tummy ache? Does your belly feel full and sore? Then chamomile is the herb for you! The doctors in France and Spain recognize chamomile as a valuable children's herb for colic, upset stomach and sleeplessness.

A cup of chamomile tea soothes the stomach, helps digestion and gets rid of gas. It even helps stop colic in babies. In fact, drinking chamomile tea every day can regulate your bowel movements, too. You can also add 1 teaspoon lemon balm and 1/4 teaspoon ginger to 2 teaspoons chamomile to make your tummy really smile!

OUCH! MY NEW TEETH ARE COMING IN!

Chamomile has important nutrients for the bones and nerves. Because of this, it helps teeth grow. When you are getting new teeth, drink a lot of chamomile tea. This will help you feel better and aids new teeth coming in.

Chamomile also helps heal any other illnesses which can occur during teething—such as earaches, stomachaches and fevers.

CALM THAT COLIC

Does a baby you know cry a lot from colic? Help your mom or dad ease its discomfort by giving baby 1/4-1/2 teaspoon of chamomile tea every few hours. You can also help give the baby a chamomile bath, or lay a cloth soaked in chamomile tea over his or her belly. Chamomile will help baby feel much better.

(**Note:** Never put honey in a tea for children under 2 years old, as it can make them sick.)

STORY TIME!
Chamomile's Story

Chamomile has been around as long as anyone can remember, but she has not always been as helpful as she is now. In fact, when Chamomile was very young, she was quite fussy and didn't want anyone to touch her. Whenever animals walked by, Chamomile would shrink back so they wouldn't mess up her pretty face. Since she didn't want anyone to use her flowers, Chamomile developed a bitter taste. In fact, she tasted so bad that humans stopped using her.

Over time Chamomile withdrew until she lived alone on a hill. Only the sun was her friend. *Now,* she thought, *no one can touch me or bother me.* Preening herself she would think, *I am so dainty and pretty!* Alas, no one noticed and no one seemed to care. Being so alone all the time, she grew smaller and smaller until she became invisible to all but the sun. Eventually Chamomile became so lonely, she cried and cried, wondering what to do.

One day, the sun noticed she was crying and seemed ready to change. Just at the moment when Chamomile became unbearably lonely, the sun sent a spark of light down into her heart. Zap! Suddenly Chamomile realized how vain and selfish she had been, only caring about herself and how she looked. She then realized how much better it must feel to be kind and helpful to others.

As Chamomile grew happier and happier with these thoughts, the bitterness from her flowers began to disappear until all that was left was a mild pleasant apple-like flavor that people would like. Only the faintest trace of her bitterness remained to remind her of the time she had withdrawn from everyone, making herself bitter and lonely. She then developed "tolerance" power inside herself. By doing that she was less fussy, and could help others feel less fussy, too.

Further, Chamomile decided to welcome people by letting them step on her. Now she enjoys being touched and used by all who need her healing medicine. Today Chamomile is a happy plant with many important uses for her human friends.

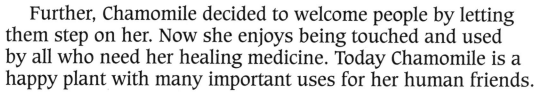

SECRET HERBAL HAIR RINSE

Chamomile has been used for hundreds of years as a hair rinse. If used regularly over time, it can lighten blond hair. Just make chamomile tea, and after you shampoo and rinse your hair, pour the cooled tea over your head. Dry and see your hair glow!

Note: *If you have dark hair, use rosemary instead. It also has been used for a long time as a hair rinse.*

SKIN TROUBLES?

Chamomile is excellent for the skin. It heals burns, cuts, scrapes, rashes and even diaper rash for your baby brother or sister. Just apply the herb as a poultice and watch your skin heal. (See the herb plantain for how to make a poultice.) You can also wash the affected area with chamomile tea and let it air dry. Sprinkling powdered chamomile on irritated skin works, too.

TOO MANY SWEETS?

If your stomach feels upset after eating too much sugar, then drink a cup of chamomile tea. It will ease your discomfort and help rebalance your body after having too many sweets. It also helps lessen cravings for sweets.

COMFREY
The Knitbone Herb

Comfrey has the unique ability to join skin and bones together. It does this by causing cells to grow which bind torn skin or broken bones. Because of this, it is often known by its nickname, knitbone, for it helps "knit" skin or bones together.

USE COMFREY FOR:

* skin tears, wounds, scrapes, sores, burns, boils, cuts, splinters
* eczema
* broken/fractured bones
* sprains, swellings, bruises
* spider bites, bee stings
* bleeding
* tonsillitis
* sore throat

Latin Name: *Symphytum officinalis*
Parts Used: leaves and root
Energy and Taste: cold energy; bitter taste
Dose for Children: Do not use comfrey internally. However, it is safe to put on their skin, and you can use as much as you need.
Make as a: wash, poultice, salve, oil, bath, powder, fomentation, foot bath, foot powder, baby powder, liniment, lip balm, eyewash.

Comfrey Plant

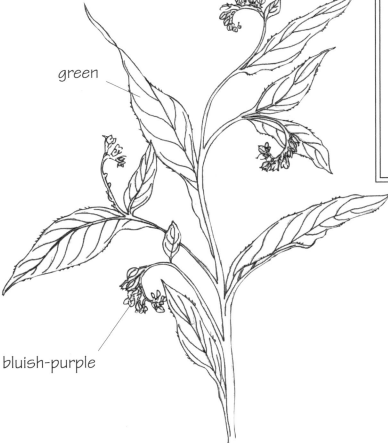

green

bluish-purple

BONEHEAL!

Did you break or fracture a bone? Then help it heal quickly by applying a comfrey poultice or fomentation to the skin area on top of the fracture or break. (See plantain for making poultices and ginger for making fomentations.)

SALVES

A salve is an herbal oil hardened with the addition of just the right amount of beeswax. It is spread on the skin to heal cuts, scrapes, bruises, wounds, sores and other skin irritations, eruptions and infections.

* Combine 1½ ounces dried or powdered herbs or 3 ounces fresh herbs with 1 cup olive or sesame oil in a pan.

* Simmer over low heat for 20 minutes.

* Melt 1/2- ounce beeswax carefully in another pan and pour into the herbal oil. Mix well.

* Add 1/8 teaspoon vitamin E oil to preserve the oil.

* Test for consistency: dip a teaspoon into the oil and either blow on it gently or place it in the refrigerator until the oil gets hard, about 3-5 minutes. If it is too hard, add more oil; if too soft, add more beeswax. Do this until you get the mix just right.

* Pour the oil into a small jar or tin and cover tightly.

Herbs to use: comfrey, plantain, echinacea (coneflower), mullein, lemon balm, yarrow, calendula, slippery elm, elder.

An excellent herbal salve for healing most skin problems, including mosquito bites, can be made by combining equal parts of these herbs: comfrey, plantain, elder, echinacea, calendula and chickweed (chickweed stops itching).

MAGICAL LIP BALM

Use comfrey salve for a lip balm! It not only soothes your lips, but quickly heals cuts and chapped, sore lips. You can make different flavors by adding a drop of your favorite flavoring extract or essential oil. Try adding a little stevia with your flavoring extract to make a sweet lip balm. (Stevia is a plant that is naturally sweet-tasting.) Or mix 2 teaspoons honey into the salve oil before adding the beeswax.

THE ENCHANTED HERB

Comfrey comforts your skin because when mashed it is gummy and slippery. It is this same substance that helps knit torn skin together. A salve made only from comfrey leaves is excellent for healing all cuts, bruises, sores, wounds, burns, stings, scrapes, skin breaks, boils and bites. The results are very quick and quite spectacular — enchanting!

Like plantain, comfrey helps ease the sting from bees. It also draws out the stinger as well as splinters, the poison from spider bites and pus from boils. Use a salve, poultice (see the poultice instructions under plantain), or saturate a cotton ball in comfrey tea and tape in place. You can also open a capsule of comfrey powder, mix the powder with water and tape in place. Change the poultice or cotton ball several times throughout the day.

DID YOU KNOW . . .

§ In the Middle Ages comfrey was a famous remedy for broken bones. It was widely cultivated in gardens for this and for its ability to heal wounds quickly. The ancient Greeks and Romans used it to treat cuts, burns, wounds and skin irritations.

§ Pouring comfrey tincture into a wound often closes it, thus avoiding the need for stitches. It may sting at first, but causes far less pain than stitches.

TOUCH AND FEEL

Get down on the ground near a comfrey plant. Very carefully look up and under its leaves. Can you see the tiny prickles under the leaves? Now gently touch the bottom of a leaf. What does it feel like?

Break a small leaf off its stem. Look inside the stem and feel the liquid there. Do you feel the slippery juices inside? This is the healing substance of the leaves. (It's called allantoin: a-lan-tow-in).

95

STORY TIME!
The Knitbones

Long ago, a magical tribe of tiny people lived in the woods. Called the Knitbones, they helped heal wounded animals. When an animal was hurt, the Knitbones climbed onto the animal and surrounded the wound. Then they put their hands together and began to chant: "Comfrey, comfrey, heal me! Make me strong and well again." Slowly a soft milky-white fiber spun from their hands, not unlike a spider's silky web. This wove new skin over the wound and knit any broken bones together.

The Knitbones and animals lived together peacefully until more and more humans moved into the woods and cut down many of the trees. This destroyed the animals' homes. Finally, many animals had to leave to find new woods in which to live.

Soon the Knitbones knew they couldn't survive much longer. They needed to use their healing power in a new way. After much thought, they decided on a plan. With one last look at their woods, all the Knitbones climbed onto the

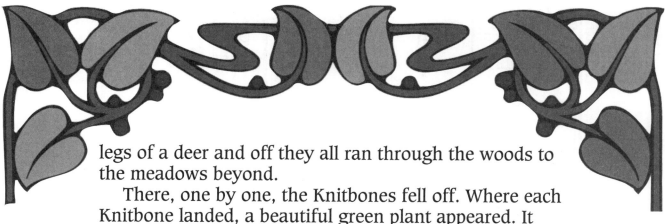

legs of a deer and off they all ran through the woods to the meadows beyond.

There, one by one, the Knitbones fell off. Where each Knitbone landed, a beautiful green plant appeared. It had a thick deep root and broad green leaves. Whenever healing was needed, the leaf was mashed and put on the wound. When the leaves were mashed, a slippery substance appeared, very much like the fiber the Knitbones spun during their healings.

Ever since then people have called this plant the Knitbone herb. We also know it by its common name, comfrey. When we use the leaves or root, its medicine heals broken bones, ligaments and tissues. It works so fast you can almost watch new skin grow. Thanks to the Knitbones, we have this wonderful herb today.

Comfrey Song

Michael Tierra

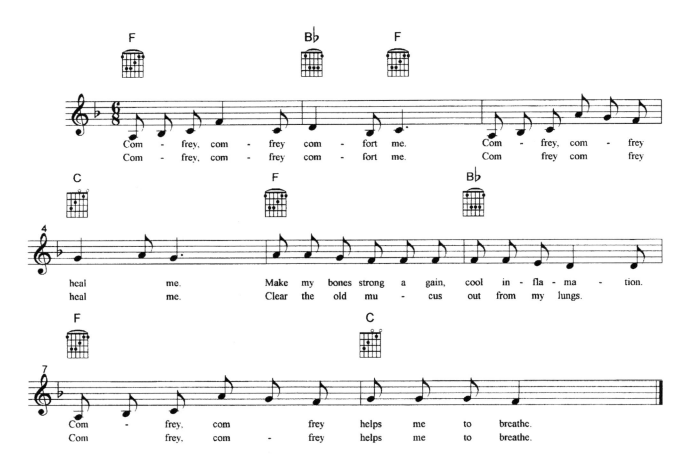

SLIPPERY ELM
The Stomach-Soothing Bark

The inner bark of the slippery elm tree is a highly nutritious food-herb. It is wonderfully strengthening and healing with many valuable uses.

Slippery Elm Tree

brown

green

brown

green

USE SLIPPERY ELM FOR:

* a nutritious food
* nausea, vomiting
* inflammation of stomach, intestines and bladder
* bronchitis, pleurisy
* sore and dry throat
* dry skin, chapped lips
* coughs
* bleeding from the lungs or colon
* ulcers
* swollen glands
* dysentery, diarrhea
* wounds, boils, ulcers, burns, rashes
* diaper rash

Latin Name: *Ullmus fulva*
Part Used: inner bark of the slippery elm tree
Energy and Taste: neutral energy; sweet taste
Dose for Children: This is a very mild and safe herb. You can eat a bowl of porridge 3 times a day if you want, take 2 pills 3 times a day, or ingest up to 1/2 ounce of the powder a day.
Make as a: tea, powder, poultice, food, syrup, salve, pill, milk, paste, capsule, wash, oil, foot powder, baby powder, lip balm.

SOOTHING FOOT POWDERS

A foot powder is a powder sprinkled on your toes and feet to heal any skin problems or make your feet smell good. It's that simple!

Slippery elm makes a fine foot powder because it is so soothing to the skin. It heals wounds, burns, boils and rashes of all sorts. If you itch between your toes, sprinkle slippery elm powder between them and feel those itches quickly fade away. Also, slippery elm smells pleasantly sweet, which is why it makes your feet smell good, too!

Herbs to Use: *slippery elm, comfrey, plantain, calendula, echinacea (coneflower), elder.*

DID YOU KNOW . . .
There is as much nutrition in slippery elm as there is in a bowl of oatmeal. Eating slippery elm during any kind of sickness is not only healing, but strengthening as well.

HERBAL PILLS

Don't you just hate pills? Aren't they huge and hard to swallow? Well, now say goodbye to that problem. When you create your own herbal pills, you can make them any size you want—as tiny as a pea or even smaller! And if they have slippery elm in them, they simply slip down your throat with ease.

Herbal pills are made entirely of herbs with a small binder added to hold everything together. Slippery elm is quite often used as that binder. Pills can be swallowed, or dissolved slowly in the mouth like a lozenge. Store in a tightly covered glass container in a cool, dark, dry place for up to a year.

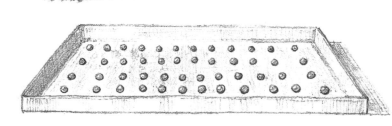

- Powder 1 oz. herb(s) in a nut and seed or coffee grinder, or in a food processor. Mix together.

- Add 1/4 ounce binder (slippery elm or whole wheat flour).

- Slowly add enough water to form a dough. (Caution: Dough that is too wet takes longer to dry!)

- Roll the dough into little balls about the size of a pea. Space evenly apart on a cookie sheet.

- Place the uncovered cookie sheet in warm air away from windows for about 10 hours. Or put the cookie sheet in an oven on low heat (250 degrees F.) for about 1-2 hours, until dry.

Secret Pill Formulas:

Sore throat and coughs: slippery elm, mullein, echinacea (coneflower), licorice, elder and ginger

Digestive Aid: slippery elm, lemon balm, fennel, ginger and chamomile

Colds, flu: lemon balm, echinacea (coneflower), yarrow, elder and ginger

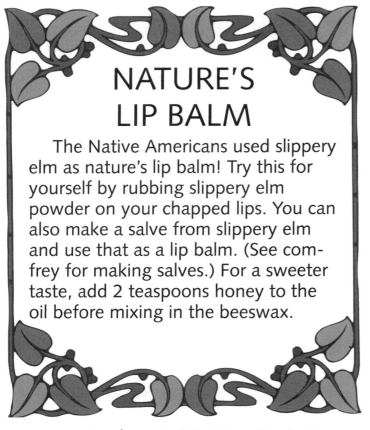

NATURE'S LIP BALM

The Native Americans used slippery elm as nature's lip balm! Try this for yourself by rubbing slippery elm powder on your chapped lips. You can also make a salve from slippery elm and use that as a lip balm. (See comfrey for making salves.) For a sweeter taste, add 2 teaspoons honey to the oil before mixing in the beeswax.

HEAL YOUR SKIN WITH PASTE!

Now this isn't the paste you use as glue! It is a paste made from slippery elm powder. This paste is actually called a poultice. It quickly heals sores, rashes, burns, boils and inflamed and infected skin.

* Mix slippery elm powder with enough water to form a paste.

* Smear on the affected area.

* Bandage and leave in place.

* Change the paste and bandage several times throughout the day until the problem has gone away.

SLIPPERY ELM PORRIDGE

If you ever feel so sick or nauseous that you can't eat or keep down any food, then eat this porridge. Slippery elm is the one food that you'll be able to eat. It will also stop you from throwing up.

This is because slippery elm is very soothing to the stomach, curing upset stomachs, vomiting and nausea. It is also a nutritious food for infants and sick people. Besides, it tastes pleasantly sweet as well!

* Mix 2 tablespoons slippery elm powder with 1/4 teaspoon cinnamon and 3 tablespoons cold water to form a smooth paste.

* Slowly add 3/4 cup cold water, stirring constantly to prevent lumps. (If it lumps up, blend in a blender or food processor.)

* Slowly heat the mixture, stirring frequently.

* Let cool. If desired, add in 1/2-1 teaspoon honey for extra sweetness. You may also add one of these: 1/4 teaspoon ginger, cardamom, nutmeg or lemon rind.

* This porridge has a slippery texture, but a pleasant flavor.

SLIPPERY ELM LOZENGES

Slippery elm lozenges soothe sore and dry throats quickly. They also help heal dry coughs and other lung ailments.

- Make a tea of licorice using 1/2 cup water and 1 teaspoon chopped licorice root. Simmer covered for 10 minutes, then strain. You should have 1/4 cup tea. If less, add a little water to make 1/4 cup liquid.

- Put 1/2 cup slippery elm powder in a bowl and make a hole in the center. Pour 1/4 cup tea (or plain water if you don't have licorice tea) into the hole and gently mix into the slippery elm powder to make a smooth dough.

- Sprinkle some slippery elm powder on a clean flat surface and roll out the dough to 1/4 inch thickness.

- Cut lozenges into small circles - a tiny bottle cap, such as the lid from a vanilla extract bottle works well. Or roll dough into small balls, flatten and smooth the edges with your fingers. Make sure all the edges are very smooth so the lozenges aren't sharp when you suck on them. You can press designs into each lozenge if you like.

- Set evenly spaced on a plate. Leave out uncovered overnight or for a day or two until completely hardened.

- Store in a dark bottle or tin in a cool, dry, dark place.

- Suck on the pill so it dissolves in your mouth and coats your throat to heal your throat and lungs.

NOTE: For even stronger-acting lozenges, use 1/2 cup cough syrup you have already made (see licorice for how to make a syrup). Try using licorice, elder, ginger and echinacea (coneflower) for the syrup.

STORY TIME!
The Magic Bird's Gift

ong ago in a faraway kingdom there lived a queen and her young son. The queen's husband had died a few years earlier and she was lonely. One day she met a man who charmed her and her courtiers. They were married and ruled the kingdom together. The new king acted kind and generous, but he had everyone fooled, for actually he was quite cruel and evil. He plotted to take over the kingdom in secret, doing so slowly and quietly.

When the queen's son grew to be a young man, his evil stepfather decided it was time to get rid of him. Daily he had a small portion of a slow-acting poison put in the prince's food or drink. At first the prince felt a little odd, then he felt ill. Over time he grew so sick he couldn't even get out of bed. He threw up day and night. The royal physicians tried every cure, but of course nothing worked, for the evil king was still poisoning the young prince every day.

Soon the prince knew he was dying. He was concerned for his mother and the kingdom. Using all his last strength the young man cried out to the Creator of life for help. He asked to be healed not just for himself, but for his mother and the kingdom as well.

Slowly, softly, the sound of beating wings filled the air. It grew louder, catching the prince's attention even in his weakened state. Looking out the window by his bed, the prince saw a magic dove flying near the castle. When the prince was alone in his room, the dove flew through the window and dropped something into the prince's lap. The magic dove then told the prince about the evil king and the poison. It told the boy to eat his gift and then, its wings fluttering, the dove flew out through the window.

The prince stared at the object in wonderment. It was a large piece of bark from a tree he had never seen before. He smelled the

104

slight sweetness of its inner bark and felt drawn to eat it. The prince pulled the fibers off the inside bark and chewed them. Immediately he began to feel a little bit better.

Every day the magic dove brought the prince a piece of the healing bark. The prince grew stronger, able to eat and keep food down. He insisted all food and drink be tasted first so he would no longer be poisoned. When the prince was well once more, he revealed the evil king's plot to his mother and her officials. Instantly the king was banished from the kingdom.

Then the young prince went in search of the tree whose bark had healed him. Suddenly the magic dove swooped out of the sky and dropped a tail feather near a tall tree. Looking up, the prince recognized the bark. The magic dove had shown him the slippery elm tree, the great healer.

NATURAL BABY POWDER

If you know any babies who have diaper rash, here is a quick and sure remedy:

- Wash and dry baby's bottom.
- Sprinkle slippery elm powder on the rash.
- Put on a clean diaper.
- Sprinkle more slippery elm powder on the rash every time the diaper is changed.

Other Herbs to Use: *Comfrey, plantain, elder or calendula powders may also be used.*

TOO SKINNY?

Then drink slippery elm milk! This delicious milk is highly nutritious and will help you gain weight.

- Measure 1 cup milk into a pot or pan.
- Warm milk to scalding.
- Add 1-2 teaspoons slippery elm powder.
- Sprinkle in a dash of ginger or cinnamon.
- Sweeten with honey, if desired. (Barley malt syrup is an even better choice for nutritious weight gain.)

106

ECHINACEA (Coneflower)
Nature's Infection Fighter

Echinacea (coneflower) is a beautiful garden flower found growing all over the United States. Yet, it is far more useful than just as a pretty garden plant. It is a powerful medicine, too. Echinacea is a natural antibiotic. It helps your immune system to heal infections and inflammations quickly. It also lowers fevers and fights off colds. While new teeth are coming in, you can squirt several drops of the tincture on your sore gums. If you have a sore throat, gargle with the tea, or squirt the tincture on your throat.

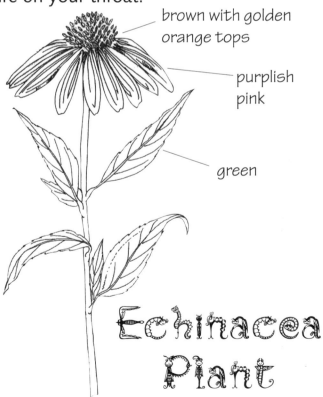

brown with golden orange tops

purplish pink

green

Echinacea Plant

USE ECHINACEA (CONEFLOWER) FOR . . .

* infections
* inflammations
* wounds
* poison oak and ivy
* fevers
* boils and other skin infections
* colds
* teething
* blood poisoning
* bites from insects, spiders, snakes

Latin Name: *Echinacea pallida, E. purpurea* and *E. angustifolia*

Part Used: usually the root, but the entire plant can be used

Energy and Taste: cool energy, bitter and pungent tastes

Dose for Children: Take 15 to 30 drops of the tincture or two "O" capsules every hour. As the symptoms lessen, reduce the frequency to every two hours, then every four hours, until the problem is gone. After all the symptoms are gone, continue taking it three times daily for another three days.

Note: Echinacea (coneflower) is a very safe herb. As you can see from the dosage, you can take a lot of it. However, for echinacea to work best, it's important to take small doses very frequently until the condition has cleared. If you don't see the condition improving in a day or two, seek professional medical help.

Make as a: tea, tincture, powder, poultice, pill, capsule, wash, mouthwash, salve, eyewash, gargle, powder, bitters, syrup, ear drops, fomentation, tooth powder, foot powder.

THE NATURAL "ANTIBIOTIC"

Echinacea (coneflower) acts like a natural antibiotic because it quickly heals infections and inflammations. It does this by stimulating the body's ability to fight off disease-causing bacteria.

To use echinacea as a natural antibiotic, do one of the following:

- Use echinacea tea as a wash on wounds, or dilute 1/4 ounce echinacea tincture in one ounce of water and use that as a wash.

- Squirt echinacea tincture on any infections or soak a cotton ball with the tincture and tape to the area. You can also take the tincture internally.

- Gargle with echinacea tea to relieve a sore throat.

- For bee stings, saturate a cotton ball with echinacea tea or tincture and tape over the wound.

BELIEVE IT OR NOT

Did you know that scientific studies have proven the powerful immune-stimulating properties of this purple daisy-like herb? It works best if taken at the very first sign of colds, flu, coughs, runny nose or scratchy throat. It will also help shorten the duration of a cold or flu.

It's very important to take echinacea (coneflower) frequently for it to work well. For best results, take 1/2 teaspoon of the tincture in water every hour until the symptoms lessen. Then take it every two hours, slowly decreasing this dosage until the problem is gone.

YIKES! A BITE!

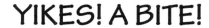

Have you ever been bitten by a spider? An ant? A flying insect? A snake? Then you know what a nasty wound they can leave.

Echinacea is the perfect herb for healing these bites. It cleanses the blood of poisons quickly and clears the infection. (Be sure to seek medical care if the bite is poisonous.)

Squirt a few drops of echinacea tincture on a cotton ball and tape over the bite. Or apply a paste of powdered echinacea mixed with a little water. Then cover with a bandage. Change with a new soaked cotton ball or paste every several hours. Any pain or discomfort will disappear and the bite will heal quickly.

PLANT SOME SEEDS

Grow coneflowers in your garden. This herb grows naturally on the Great Plains of North America. It loves sunlight. Although it dies down in winter, it comes back in the spring year after year, even after being snowed on or frozen over.

Coneflower is often grown just for its beauty. In fact, most gardeners don't even know the many valuable uses of this beautiful herb they may already have growing in their own yard. Next time you see coneflower growing in the yard of a neighbor or friend, be sure to tell them all about its many uses.

CLOSE VIEW

Use a magnifying glass to get a closer look into a coneflower. Look at all the variations of color in the petals. Now look deeply into the cone on top of the flower. What does it look like to you? Look into and between the spokes of the cone. Can you imagine why bees love these beautiful flowers so much?

SECRET REMEDY: TOOTHACHE ROOT

The Native Americans called echinacea (coneflower) toothache root because they chewed it to heal their toothaches. You can also chew a piece of the root to ease a toothache or the pain of new teeth coming in. But echinacea tincture works just as well and tastes much better!

CONEFLOWER, ECHINACEA'S OTHER NAME

Most people know the beautiful garden flower, echinacea, by its common name of coneflower. Yet in the world of herbs, coneflower is usually known by its Latin name, echinacea. When you purchase the herb at a store, or any of its products such as teas, tinctures, capsules, powder or salves, it will be labeled as echinacea and not coneflower. This is one time when it is important to know both names of the plant.

DID YOU KNOW . . .

Echinacea (coneflower) was considered one of ten sacred herbs by the Lakota Sioux. It was given to the Lakota by bear. The herbs were hanging from his claws.

POWDERING HERBS

f you want to make herbal tinctures, pills or capsules, then you need to powder the herbs first. This is simple to do:

* Place the dried herbs in a nut and seed or coffee grinder, a blender or a food processor. Grind to a fine powder. Tougher plant parts require a powerful grinder or food processor. You may need to sift the powder through a sieve, then re-grind any big pieces that remain.

* Many herbs may be purchased already powdered. However, these lose their potency quickly when exposed to air. Use powdered herbs within 6 months of being powdered.

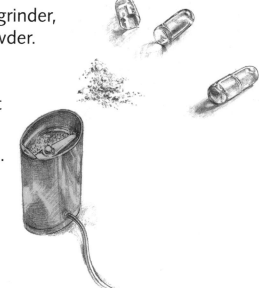

TINCTURES

 tincture is a concentrated liquid form of taking an herb. The liquids used are alcohol, glycerin or vinegar. The best tinctures for children are made with glycerin, since it is sweet-tasting and doesn't contain any alcohol. A glycerin tincture is called a glycerite. You can purchase non-synthetic vegetable glycerin at health food stores or drug stores.

(NOTE: Glycerin is so sweet that diabetics might need to count it as a sugar serving!)

Glycerites are useful for sweetening bitter-tasting herbs. They are also good when you need to take a lot of herbs over a longer period of time. Glycerites are easy to take: just squirt a few drops in your mouth or on the desired area every few hours. Then watch the problem go away. (And if you still don't like the taste, squirt it into some water and drink it that way instead.)

Glycerites are usually stored in small bottles and so travel anywhere easily, even in your pocket. Then, when you need to take your herbs, wherever you are, you can pull out your tincture and squirt a few drops into your mouth. Glycerites keep from 1-3 years if stored in a cool, dark place.

If you use an alcoholic tincture, then you can evaporate off some of the alcohol first by putting the tincture in water and boiling it for 20 minutes. Cool and drink the water.

To make a glycerite:

* Use either fresh or dried herbs. If using fresh herbs, skip the next step.
* Powder the dried herbs you want in a nut and seed or coffee grinder, a blender, or a food processor. You may also purchase powdered herbs.
* Place 2 ounces powdered herbs or 4 ounces fresh herbs in a glass jar and add 1/2 cup non-synthetic vegetable glycerin and 1/4 cup water to the jar. Mix well, then cap tightly. (Blend fresh herbs with water and glycerin in a food processor first for best results.) Make sure the herbs are covered by about a 1 inch layer of liquid. If not, add more glycerin and water.
* Shake the bottle for a minute every day to mix the herbs and liquid. Leave for 2 weeks.
* Strain the glycerite: place a cotton cloth in a colander and set in a big bowl. Pour the tincture into the cloth. Squeeze the herbs in the cloth to get out any remaining liquid.
* Throw the herbs away or compost them and strain the liquid left in the bowl a second time.
* Pour the tincture into a glass bottle and cap. Label and date.
* Store in a dark, dry place out of the sunlight. It should last from 1-3 years.

SWIMMER'S EAR

Do you love to swim but get an earache later from the water caught in your ear? Don't let that spoil your fun. Instead, squirt 2 to 4 drops of echinacea tincture (the adult tincture made with alcohol) into each ear right after you get out of the water. Make sure you let the drops sink into your ear for a few minutes so the alcohol can evaporate the water before you put the drops into your other ear.

NOTE: Do not use if you suspect a punctured eardrum.

MOUTHWASH AND GARGLE

A mouthwash cleanses the mouth, heals infections and strengthens the gums. It is swished around in the mouth and then spat out. A gargle heals sore and inflamed throats.

♦ Simmer 1 ounce herbs to 2 cups water for 20-30 minutes, until 1 cup of tea remains.

♦ Cool. Rinse your mouth or gargle with the tea as needed.

Mouthwash - Herbs to use: echinacea (coneflower), yarrow, parsley, ginger, chamomile. (The herb myrrh is good, too.)

Gargle - Herbs to use: echinacea (coneflower), ginger, licorice, calendula, elder.

SHOT SHOCK

Vaccinations and immunizations can be a shock to your body. To ease their aftereffects, take 1/2 teaspoon echinacea tincture every hour for 24 hours after you get a vaccination or immunization.

Echinacea Song

Michael Tierra

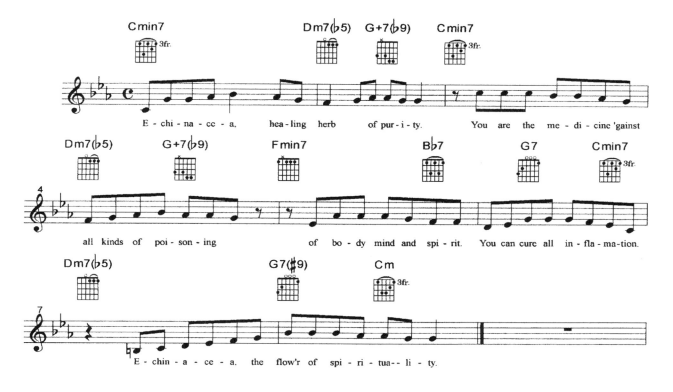

STORY TIME!
Purple Coneflower

n the outskirts of a small village a woman named Maria lived with her small child. Her husband had died the year before, and left them in the care of the village. The people of the village provided her with food after their hunts, and in return, she supplied them with beautiful hand-woven baskets.

One day Maria's child fell very ill. She tried everything she knew to get her well, but nothing worked. She sought out neighbors for help, and found many of the villagers were sick with the same strange illness her child had. All known cures had failed and even the medicine people couldn't heal them. In despair, Maria fled to her special spot in nature, a tall tree on the Great Plains near her village. She was so upset at the number of people sick from the strange disease that she cried all the way to the tree.

When Maria arrived, she immediately began praying, "Oh, Great Spirit, Creator of all Life, thank you for your many gifts of food, water and shelter. But there is a great sickness in my village which no one can cure. My child is sick as well. Please! Help us! Send a cure so that my child and people may live!"

Maria fell silent, waiting for an answer. After a while she heard a small voice inside of her say, "Because you have prayed not just for yourself, but for others as well, the cure has been sent. Go! Wherever your tears have fallen you will find a beautiful purple flower. Make a tea of the whole plant and give it to everyone who is sick. They will all get well again."

Turning, Maria saw a trail of beautiful pink-purple flowers with a big sparkly cone in the center. These flowers reached all the way to her village. She picked as many plants and roots as she could carry, leaving about two-thirds of them so they could reseed themselves and grow back each year. When Maria arrived home, she washed the plants and roots well and stuffed a pot full of them. She added hot water to the pot to make a tea. When the tea was brewed, she gave a cup to her child, and then carried more to all the ill people in the village.

Soon the villagers were well again. Rejoicing, they thanked the Great Spirit for sending the new plant to cure them. They named the herb Purple Coneflower, after the shape of its flower head. People have used it ever since. Some even carry a piece of coneflower root with them on long journeys, both for good luck and for medicine. Today we know this herb as echinacea. It is still a great remedy for all people as it heals many illnesses.

LICORICE
The Peacemaker Herb

Don't you just love chewing on a licorice rope? Traditionally these are made from licorice syrup. Have you ever chewed on a real licorice stick? It is from the root of the licorice plant and is full of that delicious licorice taste. It has many healing powers, too, as it is a very soothing and calming herb.

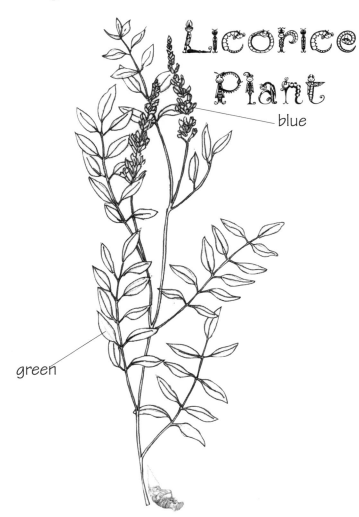

Licorice Plant

— blue

green

USE LICORICE FOR:

* coughs
* sore throats
* laryngitis
* bronchitis
* mucus congestion
* thirst
* ulcers
* spasms
* poor digestion
* low energy
* calming, relaxing
* flavoring

Latin Name: *Glycyrrhiza glabra*
Part Used: root
Energy and Taste: neutral energy; pleasant taste
Dose for Children: You can eat up to 5 licorice pills, chew on 2 licorice sticks or drink one cup of licorice tea a day. Be careful, because taking more licorice than this can upset your stomach.
Make as a: tea, pill, paste, syrup, gargle, milk, cider, sun tea, powder, capsule, spice, candy, tooth powder, mouthwash, food.

BELIEVE IT OR NOT!

The chief active part of licorice is fifty times sweeter than cane sugar! Further, it eases thirst, while sugar causes thirst. Also, licorice relieves inflammations, while sugar makes them worse.

SYRUPS

A syrup is used to treat coughs, bronchitis, colds, flu, mucus congestion and sore throats. It is soothing to the throat and lungs and a delicious way to take herbs. Syrups keep about a month in the refrigerator. Take a teaspoon of the syrup as needed.

* Make a tea of your desired herbs, using 1/2 cup of herbs to 2 cups water.

* Simmer the roots for 15 minutes in a covered pan. Then add flowers and/or leaves and steep covered for another 20 minutes.

* Strain. While still warm, add 1/2 cup of honey or glycerin. Stir well until dissolved.

* Cool, then pour into a glass bottle with a tight lid. Refrigerate.

Herbs to Use: *Licorice, ginger, garlic, mullein, elder, plantain, lemon balm, cinnamon, fennel, a pinch of cayenne.*

MAGICAL THROAT COAT

Licorice is very soothing for sore throats and stomachaches. It also quiets coughs and helps cure colds and flu. There are two good ways to take it for these conditions. One is as a throat lozenge pill (see slippery elm for making lozenges); another is as a syrup.

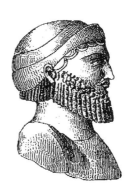

HAPPY CAMPER

In ancient Greece licorice was used to quench thirst. If you are traveling or hiking, licorice roots are good to take along. When you get thirsty you can chew on one

TEETHING ROOT

Licorice root is a delicious way to help ease the pain of teething. Pound one end of a licorice stick to separate the fibers. Then use as a chewing stick for toothache, teething or cleaning the teeth.

STRESS-FREE TEA

Licorice tea is very calming, creating a peaceful feeling. It is especially good for soothing stress.

This tea is full of the delicious licorice taste. It is sweet all by itself and doesn't need anything added. In fact, licorice is often added to other teas as a natural sweetener.

🍃 Simmer in a covered pot two whole slices (or one teaspoon chopped) licorice in one cup water for 20 minutes.

🍃 Strain, cool and drink.

Note: For a relaxing tea, add chamomile.

DID YOU KNOW . . .

☞ Licorice is the most commonly used herb in China. It is called "peacemaker herb" and is added to most herbal formulas to help all the herbs work together.

☞ Licorice is taken as a tea in some monasteries to help quiet the mind for meditation.

STORY TIME!
Cory and Fishwort

Long ago in a small village there once lived a man with a long hook nose and a big wart on his chin. Since he looked strange, people called him Fishwort behind his back. Whenever he heard them call him names, it made him feel unhappy and lonely.

One day Fishwort discovered a magic potion that would make anyone who drank it become his slave. He gave the potion to all the villagers and soon they were pleading to be his slaves. Now Fishwort didn't feel lonely.

The villagers worked for Fishwort day and night. They were so busy, children could no longer play games nor parents visit with each other. Every evening Fishwort brewed the magic potion. Then first thing the next morning he gave it to the villagers to drink.

One morning a young girl named Cory was picking berries in the woods when the drink was given. Now it just so happened that when she ate some berries, the evil spell over her was broken. When she returned to the village Cory was shocked to see how hard all the villagers slaved under Fishwort's spell. In vain she tried to tell them about the magic potion, but no one believed her.

Every day Cory escaped drinking the potion, but could not get anyone else to stop. When Fishwort noticed Cory was avoiding the potion and stirring up trouble, he sent several of the villagers under his spell to capture her. Just as they were about to grab her, Cory saw what Fishwort meant to do. Quickly, she ran far away. Eventually she came into the middle of a meadow where she collapsed, exhausted and sobbing.

After a long while Cory heard a tiny voice speak. "Girl, I can help you if you'd like," the gentle voice said.

Startled, Cory raised her head and wiped her eyes. Looking around, she didn't see a person in sight. "Who are you?" Cory asked. "I can't see you!"

The voice giggled, then said, "I am all around you. My body is the plant you see, but I am the spirit of that plant."

Cory gently stroked the long many-leafed plants she saw spread about her. She spilled out her story. When she was finished, the plant spirit told Cory how she could free the town and heal Fishwort.

Overjoyed, Cory immediately carried out the plan. She carefully gathered many of the plants' roots, then returned to the village that night and cooked a thick brew similar to the magic potion. The next day the root tea was given to the villagers in place of the magic potion.

Soon the townsfolk began acting normal again and became aware of their slavery. The villagers banded together and found Fishwort. Before they could punish him, Cory appeared. She explained about the magic potion, the plant spirit and the new root tea they all had been drinking.

Fishwort coughed uneasily and then said, "It's true, I do not have any special powers. I was very lonely and you wouldn't accept me. So I decided to use the magic potion to put you under my spell. I didn't mean to hurt you, but I felt terribly rejected and alone."

Everyone was stunned by the great change in Fishwort. In time the villagers began to accept him and he was no longer ridiculed and lonely. Soon everyone learned that the new herb, which had freed them from their evil spell, was also good for neutralizing poisons and creating peaceful feelings. They named it licorice, in honor of Cory. And that's how licorice came to be.

GINGER
Spice for Digestion

Have you ever eaten gingerbread cookies? The special taste and spiciness of these cookies comes from ginger. Ginger is also used to spice pumpkin pie and other foods. Yet, no matter how it is used in the kitchen, ginger is also a very healing herb.

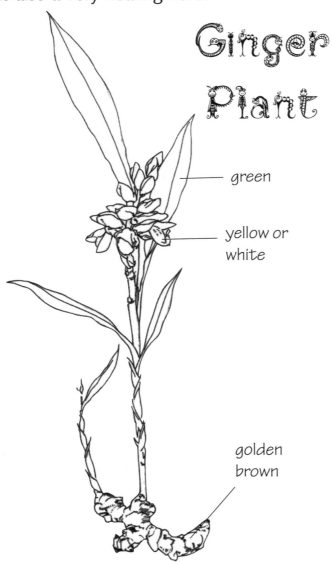

Ginger Plant

green

yellow or white

golden brown

USE GINGER FOR:

* feelings of coldness
* chills
* sore throat with feelings of coldness
* colds, flu with chills and low fever
* cough and lung congestion with clear to white mucus
* nausea, vomiting, cramps
* gas
* stomachache

Latin Name: *Zingiberis officinalis*
Part Used: the root
Energy and Taste: warm energy; spicy taste
Dose for Children: Because ginger is quite spicy and stimulating, don't drink more than 1-2 cups of ginger tea a day. For illnesses, drink 1/4 to 1/2 cup ginger tea every 2-3 hours until the symptoms lessen. Then decrease the dose to a little each day until the problem is gone.
Make as a: tea, bath, syrup, milk, spice, tincture, mouthwash, gargle, fomentation, sun tea, pill, capsule, powder, candy, liniment, bitters, foot bath, wash, paste, chai tea.

THE ENERGY OF AN HERB

Every herb has a special "energy." The energy of an herb is how it affects the body. Some herbs make us cooler, while others warm us up. This happens whether the herb is cold from the refrigerator or hot from the stove, because it is the nature of the herb to do this. Since it was created this way, the energy of an herb can never be changed, just as a dog can't become a cat, nor a flower a rock.

An herb with a cooling energy helps heal illnesses with heat, such as high fevers, red, swollen sore throats and infections. An herb with a warming energy helps heal illnesses with signs of coldness, such as a white, mucusy cough with chills, a low fever and no thirst. Just the opposite is also true. Heating herbs and foods will make hot conditions worse, while cooling things will make cold conditions worse.

Knowing the energy of an herb is important so you can choose the right herb for healing. Read Appendix 1, "Herbs and Their Energies," to learn more about this important topic.

Look up all the herbs in this chapter. What is the energy of each herb? (**Hint:** look at the "Energy and Taste" line.) What is the energy of ginger?

or ?

125

GINGER COOKIES

Because ginger is so warming and spicy, it isn't chewed raw very often. Usually it is just used in cooking. Try these delicious ginger cookies to enjoy their ginger flavor.

Bake: 18-20 minutes
Oven: 350 degrees F.
Makes: 10-12 cookies

☺ Blend until creamy: 1 stick (½ cup) butter, ¾ cup sugar

☺ Beat in: 2 eggs

☺ Sift: 2¼ cups whole wheat flour

☺ Resift with: 1 teaspoon baking soda, 1½ teaspoon powdered ginger, 1 teaspoon cinnamon, ¼ teaspoon cloves, ½ teaspoon salt, 1 tablespoon fresh, grated ginger (optional)

☺ Add sifted ingredients to butter mixture and blend.

☺ Chill dough ½ hour.

☺ Roll out dough and cut with cookie cutters or shape by hand.

☺ Place 1" apart on a buttered sheet and bake.

DID YOU KNOW . . .

☞ Ginger comes from India, but grows in tropical areas, such as Hawaii and Jamaica. It has a fragrant white or yellow flower. Sometimes the flowers are used in ornamental flower bouquets.

✳

☞ Ginger has been highly prized for centuries by the Europeans, Chinese and East Indians as a special spice with healing powers.

✳

☞ You can add ginger to your soup, vegetable and meat dishes. It adds a spicy taste while it helps digestion! Try adding a good amount of ginger to cakes, pies and cookies to increase their flavor and help in their digestion.

FOMENTATIONS

A fomentation is an herbal fluid wrapped on the body and kept warm. Sometimes it is called a compress. It benefits swellings, pains, colds, flu, congestion, sprains, coughs, cramps, pains, infections, strained muscles and poor circulation, depending on the herbs used. To make:

🖐 Make a tea out of the desired herbs.

🖐 Dip a washcloth into the tea and let it soak 5-10 minutes.

🖐 Using tongs, lift the cloth out of the tea. Quickly wring out most of the fluid.

🖐 Immediately place the cloth over the desired area. Cover with a towel, then a hot water bottle or heating pad. Cover both with a large towel or blanket to keep it warm.

🖐 Leave on 20 minutes. Repeat process if desired.

🖐 **Herbs to use:** comfrey, ginger, plantain, chamomile, yarrow, mullein, calendula, elder.

GINGER FOMENTATION

A fomentation made only of ginger is a wonderful way to ease painful joints, muscles, sprains, strains and spasms and to warm the body. It feels good on the belly, too, easing tummy aches, gas, bloating, diarrhea or poor digestion.

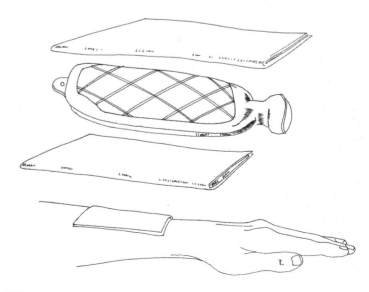

MAGICAL GINGER POTION

inger quickly eases an aching belly with cramps, gas, nausea or heartburn. Make ginger tea and drink right away. Your belly will soon feel much better! It's magical!

* Simmer three slices or 1 tablespoon grated fresh ginger in 1 cup of water for 10 minutes in a covered pot.

* Turn off the heat and let sit for 15 minutes.

* Strain, cool and drink.

* Or, add 1/4 teaspoon dried ginger to 1 cup of boiling water. Cool and drink.

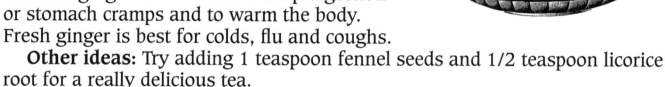

Dried ginger is best used to help digestion or stomach cramps and to warm the body. Fresh ginger is best for colds, flu and coughs.

Other ideas: Try adding 1 teaspoon fennel seeds and 1/2 teaspoon licorice root for a really delicious tea.

GINGER-ALE FIZZ

This ginger fizz tastes very much like the old-fashioned ginger ales. Try it!

1 teaspoon grated fresh ginger root, or 1/2 teaspoon ginger powder
1 cup water
1/2 cup carbonated water
2 teaspoons sugar (raw or brown sugar is preferable) or honey

* Bring ginger and water to a boil. Turn down heat to low and simmer covered for no more than 5 minutes.

* Remove from heat and let sit covered for 10 minutes. Strain.

* Add carbonated water.

* Stir in sugar or honey. Let cool.

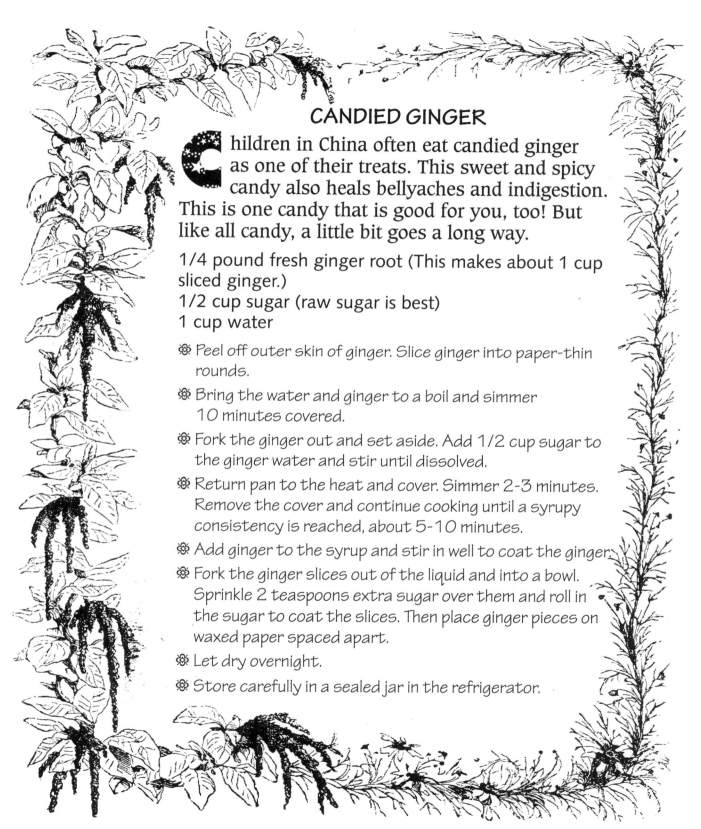

CANDIED GINGER

Children in China often eat candied ginger as one of their treats. This sweet and spicy candy also heals bellyaches and indigestion. This is one candy that is good for you, too! But like all candy, a little bit goes a long way.

1/4 pound fresh ginger root (This makes about 1 cup sliced ginger.)
1/2 cup sugar (raw sugar is best)
1 cup water

❀ Peel off outer skin of ginger. Slice ginger into paper-thin rounds.

❀ Bring the water and ginger to a boil and simmer 10 minutes covered.

❀ Fork the ginger out and set aside. Add 1/2 cup sugar to the ginger water and stir until dissolved.

❀ Return pan to the heat and cover. Simmer 2-3 minutes. Remove the cover and continue cooking until a syrupy consistency is reached, about 5-10 minutes.

❀ Add ginger to the syrup and stir in well to coat the ginger.

❀ Fork the ginger slices out of the liquid and into a bowl. Sprinkle 2 teaspoons extra sugar over them and roll in the sugar to coat the slices. Then place ginger pieces on waxed paper spaced apart.

❀ Let dry overnight.

❀ Store carefully in a sealed jar in the refrigerator.

HOT TOOTSIE BATH

Give your feet a special treat—soak them in an herbal tea! Herbal foot baths feel wonderful to the whole body. A foot bath with ginger stimulates the circulation and quickly warms you up all over. If you feel cold and chilled, or just have cold feet, then put your tootsies in some warm ginger tea. It also eases sore and aching feet! Here is a quick method:

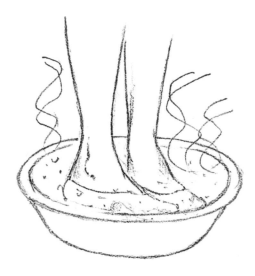

- Heat two quarts water to a boil.
- Turn off the heat and add 2 tablespoons powdered ginger (you can add 1/2 teaspoon cayenne powder, too, if you really want to warm up!).
- Stir well. Pour into a bucket, dishpan or large pot big enough for your feet to fit.
- When the tea has cooled to a very warm but tolerable temperature, stick your feet in the tea.
- Soak for 10-20 minutes.
- The tea will continue to cool down, so periodically add more hot water.

Note: You can use other herbs instead of ginger to make a foot bath. In fact, a lemon balm foot bath can help break a cold or fever! Try: roses, mint, calendula, lemon balm, sage, eucalyptus, lavender or yarrow.

CHASE THOSE SNIFFLES AWAY!

Scallion and ginger tea is very good for treating colds and clearing white and runny nasal mucus.

* Make a tea using 2 scallions (the white part) and 1 teaspoon fresh grated ginger root to one cup of water.

* Simmer covered over low heat for 10 minutes.

* Drink freely as needed.

GINGER-SESAME OIL

Rub this oil into your skin to ease the pain of achy joints, bruises or headaches. It can also be used for earaches that feel better with heat. Put 2 or 3 drops of the oil on cotton and then place the cotton in the aching ear for several hours.

Ginger-sesame oil can be massaged into the scalp and left on overnight to clear scalp diseases and dandruff (you can wash it out of your hair in the morning!). Do this 2-3 times a week. To make:

* Grate a 2" piece of fresh ginger root.

* Place gratings in a piece of cheese-cloth or other loosely woven cloth. Squeeze tightly and collect the juice in a measuring cup.

* Add an equal amount of sesame oil.

* Mix together well. Store in a sealed container in a cool, dark place. (It does not need to be refrigerated.) It keeps for several weeks.

UGH! I'M CAR-SICK!

Did you know that ginger has been found to be as effective as common over-the-counter drugs in preventing motion sickness? Ginger quickly helps to soothe an upset stomach and stop nausea and vomiting.

For best results, take one "0" or "00" capsule (see page 17 for capsule sizes) of ginger powder before you get in a car, or board a boat or plane. Be sure to keep taking the ginger capsules every hour while on the trip. Then the ginger can prevent motion sickness. If you still feel sick, or forgot to take the ginger ahead of time, take the ginger immediately to relieve your symptoms.

Ginger is also good for poor digestion and gas, as it helps your body digest food better. Its warming energy is especially good for vegetarians.

SING ALONG!

Ginger Song

Michael Tierra

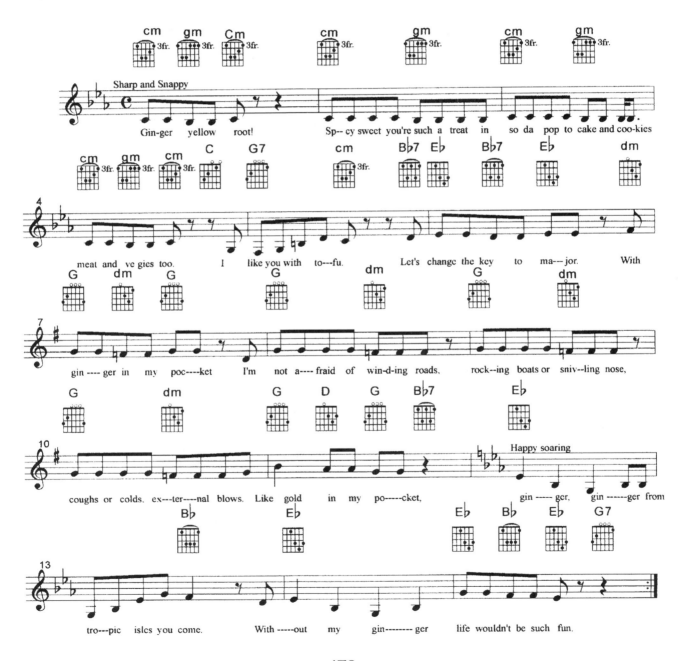

STORY TIME!
Ginger, the Golden Root

ong ago a peaceful and kindly tribe of gnomes lived deep in the earth. Theirs was a simple life as they helped one another find food, heal illness and celebrate the other joys of life.

One day a young boy gnome named Gingelgrink tunneled into a new room. In it he found some shiny yellow metal. Excitedly he showed it to all the gnomes of his tribe who lived with him in the burrows and tunnels under the ground. They had never seen anything like this strange glittering metal, so they piled it into a big hole they used for storage.

Soon the gnomes needed to travel above ground to trade with the elves for things that they couldn't find underground. This included wax for candles, wool for sweaters and a special tool to help dig tunnels in areas of particularly hard rock and dirt. When they went, they decided to take some of the yellow metal with them. When the elves saw the golden metal, they were excited and urged the gnomes to bring them more. In return, they traded for it with rare and fancy goods such as fine jewelry, colored cloth, furs and more.

Because the new goods were special and rare, many of the gnomes decided to keep the goods for themselves. They started hoarding the gold in secret piles so they could trade for more of the unusual items. Soon many people became greedy and others jealous. As a result they stopped helping each other. Eventually there were a few people with enormous riches while others were very poor.

Now, Gingelgrink, the boy gnome, watched these changes with sadness. He couldn't understand his fellow gnomes' greed

for this new metal. The tribe had certainly lived better
before the gold was found. Because he was the first
person to find the gold, he felt responsible for what
had happened. He knew he needed to find help.

Gingelgrink journeyed the old underground paths
until he found a famous sage-gnome named Trugo.
When he told Trugo what had befallen the tribe,
Trugo gave Gingelgrink special instructions about
how he could restore harmony and happiness. Then
Gingelgrink set off immediately through the long,
dark, winding burrows under the ground to his home.

When he returned, things were worse than before. There was not much food and many people sat sick and homeless. Quite a few burrows were now in such poor condition that they were collapsing and endangering the lives of everyone. Other gnomes battled endlessly over their hidden treasures. Gingelgrink knew he had to act quickly.

He went into one of the burrow-rooms and one by one, pushed each piece of gold metal into the dirt ceiling above his head. Then he cast a spell as he tossed up the rare magic dust that Trugo had given him. Suddenly a flash streaked through the entire room and all became still and silent.

The next day everyone was in an uproar—the gold had vanished! Instead, roots of a golden color grew out of their ceilings. At first they blamed each other and fought, but over time they forgot about the metal. They took down their boarded walls and started sharing what they owned again. Peace returned and the gnome tribe was both happy and healthy once more.

They discovered that the golden root tasted good, and more importantly for those who must live in the cold, damp and dark earth, it made them feel warm inside. They found they had less mucusy sniffles, fewer colds, and their bones did not ache so much. Now with their newly found golden ginger root, it was like having the warmth of the sun to offset the damp coldness of their earthy homes.

The new golden root also improved their health by easing stomachaches, nausea, colds, flu and sore throats, and by cleaning mucus from their chests. Eventually the Below People taught the Above People how to use the root. Today we call this special root ginger, and we, too, can eat it and benefit from its healing powers.

ELDER
Tree of Medicine

This ancient tree has been used by people all over the world for thousands of years. Elder is also a native shrub that grows throughout the United States. A terrific cold and flu healing herb, it fights viruses and clears chest congestion rapidly and effectively.

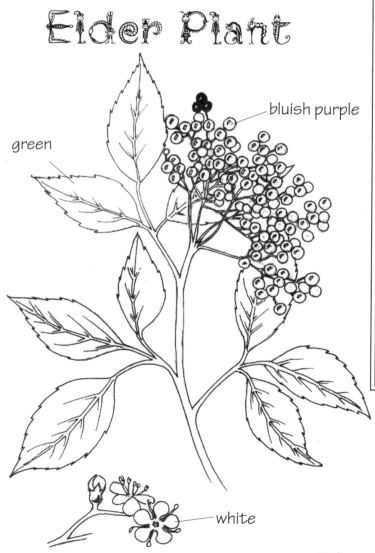

Elder Plant

green

bluish purple

white

USE ELDER FOR:
* colds, flu
* fever
* lung congestion
* sinus congestion
* hay fever
* clearing the skin
* burns
* cuts, scratches
* chapped hands
* tonsillitis
* sore throat

Latin Name: *Sambucus nigra*
Parts Used: flowers, berries
Energy and Taste: cool energy; rid and bitter tastes
Dose for Children: Drink 1/4-1/2 cup of tea every hour until the symptoms lessen. Then drink 1/2-1 cup 2 times a day until the problem has gone away. Or take 1/2-1 teaspoon syrup every 2-3 hours.
Make as a: tea, syrup, oil, salve, food, tincture, gargle, steam, wash, capsule, pill, powder and bath.
NOTE: Red elder is toxic. Only use the black elder tree.

ENCHANTED SYRUP

 lderberry syrup has been used by Europeans for centuries to prevent and relieve colds and flu. Recently, science has shown that it prevents the flu virus from invading and spreading in your body. The next time you have a cold or flu, take this syrup and you should get over it twice as fast as usual!

You will need:
1/2 cup dried elderberries
2 cups boiling water
1/2 cup honey

Pour boiling water over the elderberries, cover and let soak overnight. The next day simmer for 30 minutes. Then puree the mixture in a blender or food processor, adding the honey. Pour the syrup into a clean bottle and refrigerate. It keeps up to a month. Take 1/2-1 teaspoon every 2-3 hours. For children under the age of 2, add the syrup to hot water first to kill off any microbes in the honey that can make them sick.

FOIL THAT FLU BUG!

Next time you 'catch' a nasty flu bug, get over it fast by drinking this flu tea. Then get in bed under several covers and sweat that flu bug away!

* Steep covered for 20 minutes in 1 cup boiling water 1 teaspoon each elder, yarrow and lemon balm with 1/2 teaspoon licorice and 1-2 slices of fresh ginger.
* Strain and sweeten to taste.
* Drink 1/4-1/2 cup every 2 hours.

You could also put 3-5 drops of elder tincture into a cup of water and sip that throughout the day; better yet, take elderberry syrup!

FREEZE THOSE SNEEZES

Elder flower tea can stop sneezing from allergies, hay fever and sinus congestion. Make a tea by steeping 1 teaspoon each elder, yarrow and echinacea in 2 cups boiling water for 20 minutes. Strain, add honey to taste, and drink 1/4-1/2 cup tea every 2 hours until the sneezes are gone.

TREE OF MUSIC

 ot only has elder been called the Tree of Medicine, but also the Tree of Music! This is because people used to remove the pith from its young branches and make the hollow stems into flutes, pipes and whistles. The Romans were among those who used elder wood for making musical instruments. In England, children also used these hollowed branches for pop-guns!

DID YOU KNOW . . .

Elder is an herb well known in folk lore. There are so many legends about elder, it would take pages to write them all out. Here are a few of them:

- The Native Americans claimed that elder would heal all illnesses a person was ever likely to have. Thus, it was said to promote a long life, giving rise to its name, elder.

- In Denmark elder was connected with magic. It was said that a dryad lived in its branches and watched over the tree. Permission was always asked of the tree, called "Hylde-Maer," before cutting it down. Then the cut wood had to be made into furniture.

- Gypsies believed that burning elder wood brought bad luck.

- Russians believed that elder drove away evil spirits.

- Sicilians thought that elder wood killed serpents and drove away robbers.

- The Celtic people believed that if they stood under an elder tree on Midsummer's Eve, they would see the King of the Fairies ride past.

- Northern California Karok would cut the elder bark each year so the stalks would grow in straight, and then use them for pea shooters and play arrows for children.

- People all over the world have planted elder near their homes to protect them from evil spirits.

HERBAL CANDY DROPS

Candy drops can be good for your health, too, if they are made of healing herbs! Suck on these drops for colds, flu, chest or sinus congestion, tonsillitis and sore throats.

¼ ounce dried elder flowers (or 6 ounces fresh)

1 cup boiling water

1¾ cups sugar

½ teaspoon peppermint extract

- Pour boiling water over elder flowers and berries and let them steep 20-30 minutes, covered.

- Strain. Put tea in a very large and deep pot (this is important so the candy doesn't boil over and make a big mess).

- Add sugar and dissolve. Continue boiling (without stirring) until the mixture reaches 300-310 degrees Fahrenheit (temperature for brittle candy).

- Let sit until temperature drops to 110 degrees Fahrenheit and then stir in the peppermint extract.

- Pour the mixture quickly in $^1/_4$ teaspoon drops onto a well-buttered board or cookie sheet. Let harden.

- Store in a dry container.

- Soak the used pot and utensils in warm water to clean off the candy!

VERY BERRY!

People in Neolithic times used to eat elderberries. That was a long, long time ago! You can enjoy these dark purple elderberries today in many different ways. Cook them fresh or dried into jams, jellies, pies or pancakes. It is even said that elderberry jam is a gentle laxative! For berry tea, simmer covered 2 teaspoons berries in 1 cup water for 10 minutes. Drink 1/2 cup tea 2 times a day for colds, flu, lung congestion, constipation, or just to enjoy a very berry cup of tea!

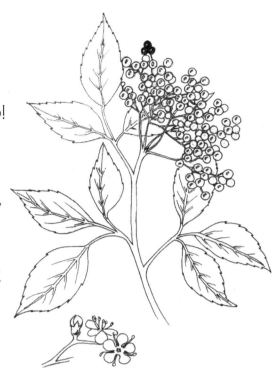

MAGICAL SKIN BALM

To soothe dry, flaky, rough, chapped or even irritated skin, rub in a bit of this balm and feel its magic work!

Make a salve from equal parts of elder, chamomile and calendula flowers. (See comfrey for making salves.)

You can also make a salve or oil of just elder flowers and put that on your skin to heal burns, cuts, scratches, sores or abrasions. (See mullein for making oils.)

EAU DE FLEUR

The ancient Egyptians first discovered that elder improves the complexion. Today in France, people use elder-flower water (*eau de sureau*) to treat dry skin. You can make your own flower-water (*eau de fleur*) and use it as a soothing rinse after washing your face.

- Place 1 teaspoon each elder, calendula and chamomile flowers in a pot.
- Pour 1 cup boiling water over the flowers and cover.
- Let sit 20 minutes.
- Strain into a clean jar and cool.
- Rinse your face with the flower-water once or twice a day and see how good it feels and how pretty it makes you look!

BEAUTY STEAM

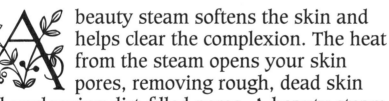

A beauty steam softens the skin and helps clear the complexion. The heat from the steam opens your skin pores, removing rough, dead skin and unclogging dirt-filled pores. A beauty steam is made the same way as an herbal steam, but herbs good for the skin are used. Be sure to add mint, some eucalyptus leaves or a drop of an essential oil such as rosemary or peppermint. This will help the other herbs penetrate the pores of your skin. (See Herbal Steams under lemon balm for steaming directions.)

Good herbs to use: elder, calendula, lemon balm, chamomile, peppermint, lavender, rosemary, yarrow, violets, rose petals, fennel.

STORY TIME
Mother Elda

Long ago there was a tiny village tucked away amid green rolling hills. Daily the children of the village walked the cobbled streets to school, waving to all their neighbors as they passed by—all of them except one, that is. In this house lived a mother and daughter, people new to the village. They lived in a small house set back from the road. The children said the house looked dark and scary, but really they were afraid of strangers.

The mother, Elda, and her daughter, Hilda, tried to make friends with the neighbors and their children. But try as they could, no one wanted to befriend them. After school was out Hilda stared longingly out the windows at the other children playing their games, but not once was she invited to join them.

Late one summer day, mother Elda saw an old, bent-over woman carrying several large parcels. Elda offered to help her. Not being from the village, the old woman gratefully followed Elda home for a bowl of soup. Elda and Hilda fed her and gave her a bed for the night. The next morning the old woman had to leave for her home. As she left, she took a small plant from one of her bags and offered it to Elda and Hilda as thanks for their kind hospitality. Hilda ran to the window to watch her leave, but was startled to find the woman was suddenly nowhere to be seen.

Hilda and her mother planted their gift in front of the house. Like magic, the plant quickly grew into a bushy tree, and then grew no more. All winter long Hilda looked at its solitary branches, bare against the gray sky. She thought it looked as lonely as she and her mother were; she even wondered if it was alive. When spring came, however, the tree soon burst out with new green leaves. These were

followed by huge white blossoms that looked like giant puff balls. It seemed the most beautiful tree Hilda had ever seen.

The following fall a terrible flu struck the village. Everyone came down with it and no known cure would heal it. The school was closed because the children and teachers were sick at home with fevers and chills. The shops were all closed as well, for their owners were in bed with terrible coughs and sore throats. No one ever had seen an illness this bad hit the village before.

Hilda also got the flu. Elda worriedly watched her toss and turn in bed, sick with a high fever. All Elda could do was hope Hilda would get well soon. Then Elda fell ill herself and had strange dreams. In one of them, the old woman who had given them the little plant came to her and told her how to make medicine and other things from the tree.

When she awoke, Elda slowly dragged herself out of bed and out to the tree. By now the white blossoms had given way to clusters of dark-purple berries. Elda picked them as she had been told in her dream. Then she went into the kitchen and made the berries into a dark rich syrup. This she gave to Hilda and then took some herself.

Within hours, both Elda and Hilda were feeling much better. They felt as if the tree had given them its magic through the beautiful berries it bore, and both knew they owed this gift to the old woman. After they were well, both Elda and Hilda took the syrup throughout the village to give to their neighbors. Within a few days, everyone was well again.

After that, Elda and Hilda became loved by all the villagers. By now their neighbors were very sorry for ignoring them and hurting their feelings. Change was difficult for the villagers, and they hadn't liked strangers. But after Elda's and Hilda's loving gift of healing, the villagers accepted them as if they were family. The children came to play with Hilda and the neighbors visited with Elda.

Elda had also learned, in her strange dream of the old woman, to take the pith out of the tree branches and make pipes, flutes and whistles for the children to enjoy. She continued to make a tea of the tree's flowers and berries to give to any of the children who had a cold or flu. Always they got well very quickly.

Great was the villagers' sorrow when Elda died one spring. Hilda buried her under the magical tree that they so loved and people from everywhere nearby came to pay their respects. Then as they had been taught by Elda, they continued to use the tree's flowers and berries for making medicine to keep the villagers strong. Before they gathered any of the tree, they always asked Elda's permission, and after a while, the villagers came to call the tree Mother Elda.

Time passed. The next generations also used the special tree until, finally, the tree came to be known as elder. Today we use this same elder tree, and it now grows all over the world. Thanks to the wonderful gift of love Elda gave to us all, you, too, can use its flowers and berries for medicine, and make flutes from its branches.

CALENDULA
(Marigold)
The Skin and Blood Herb

Calendula is a very old plant. It has been used since the twelfth century in Europe and even earlier in Egypt, where it originated. Either deep golden-yellow or orange, the calendula flower looks like the sun. It is also called pot marigold, and while different from the common marigold (Tagetes genus), it is commonly found as a favorite in most gardens.

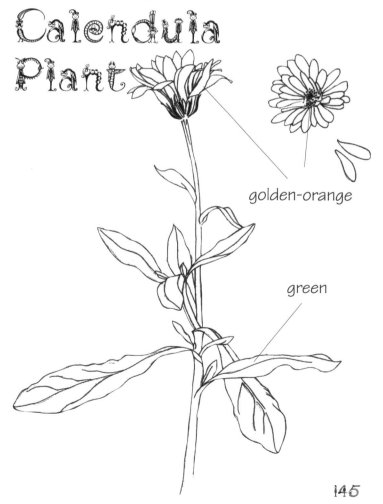

Calendula Plant

golden-orange

green

USE CALENDULA FOR:

* wounds, scrapes, cuts, sores, burns, bruises
* skin pain and irritation
* measles, chickenpox and skin eruptions
* diaper rash, cradle cap
* bee and wasp stings, insect bites
* acne, dry skin, chapped lips
* earaches
* fevers
* inflamed, sore eyes
* cramps
* ulcers
* bronchitis
* bleeding wounds
* varicose veins

Latin Name: *Calendula officinalis*
Part Used: flowers
Energy and Taste: warm energy; acrid taste
Dose for Children: Drink 1/4-1/2 cup of tea every hour until the symptoms lessen. Then drink 1/2-1 cup 2 times a day until the problem has gone.
Make as a: tea, tincture, salve, wash, ear drops, eyewash, capsule, bath, liniment, oil, pill, powder, fomentation, gargle, dried bouquet, potpourri, poultice, mouthwash, dye, sun tea, toothpowder, syrup, bitters, steam, foot bath, foot powder, baby powder, lip balm.

145

OH *NO!* THE CHICKENPOX!

hen calendula tincture is applied directly to each chickenpox spot, the itching and eruption stops immediately. It may sting at first, but the chickenpox goes away very quickly and any itching is relieved. (See echinacea for making tinctures.)

ACHY EARS?

Calendula oil heals earaches! Place 2-3 drops of calendula oil in the ear, cover with a piece of cotton and place the ear next to a hot water bottle. (See mullein for making oils.)

SKIN BALM

Calendula salve is a wonderful way to heal burns, cuts, scrapes, sores, bruises, bleeding cuts, chapped lips and diaper rash. (See comfrey for making salves and use calendula flowers instead of comfrey leaves.)

ANIMALS LIKE HERBS, TOO!

Did you know that you can cure animals with herbs, too? They respond very well and heal quickly when given herbs. Herbal teas, powders, pills and salves all work well for animals.

The next time your dog, cat, horse or other pet gets a cut, smear the salve into the area and bandage in place. Calendula salve heals wounds and stops bleeding. It is also good for bruises and sores.

GOLDEN CALENDULA POTION

A tea of calendula (marigold) brings on a sweat, breaking fevers and easing bronchitis.

To make:

* Pour boiling water over 1 tablespoon of calendula flowers.

* Cover and steep for 15-20 minutes.

* Cool, strain, add honey to taste and drink.

DID YOU KNOW . . .

* Calendula (marigold) opens and closes with the sun. On a hot day the sun pulls the resins up in the flowers, making them very sticky.

* Calendula is said to remove warts when applied directly to the wart.

DASH AWAY THOSE RASHES

Powdered calendula (marigold) mixed with a little water to form a paste can be spread on rashes and bee stings. The powder alone can be sprinkled on babies to heal or prevent diaper rash. You can also use calendula salve on any other rashes or on chapped lips. It eases any discomfort and heals them.

For acne, wash your face with cooled calendula tea, 2-3 times a day. Let air dry.

CALENDULA DYE

Did you know that cheese was originally dyed yellow with calendula flowers? Calendula was also used as a dye for cloth. You, too, can make a yellow dye and dye cloth or yarn with calendula flowers. Wool takes dyes better than cotton or other fibers, so wool yarn is best to start with.

It is best to start your yarn in what is called a "mordant bath," which "fixes" the dye and makes your wool fade-resistant. Make the mordant bath the day before you plan to dye your wool. Here is how you do it: Fill an old pot with enough water to cover your wool. Add 4 ounces alum mixed with 1 ounce cream of tartar. Bring to a boil and simmer for one hour.

Let your wool cool overnight in the mordant bath. You can immediately use the yarn for dyeing the next day, or dry and keep it until you are ready to dye it.

Note: Alum can be purchased at your local pharmacy. Cream of tartar can be found in the spice section of your supermarket. **(Keep alum away from your mouth.)**

To dye cloth or yarn:

❀ Make a large pot of calendula tea, filling the pot full of flower heads. Cover and steep for 30 minutes.

❀ Strain, keeping the liquid.

❀ Put on a pair of rubber gloves to protect your hands.

❀ Immerse the white wool cloth or yarn fully in the calendula tea. Turn on the heat and simmer 45 minutes. DO NOT BOIL.

❀ Remove the cloth or yarn with tongs. Dissolve salt in the dye bath as a color fixative. Use 1 teaspoon salt to 1 quart of dye water.

❀ Return the cloth or yarn to the dye bath and simmer for another 30 minutes (longer for darker shades). Stir occasionally with a wooden spoon. Dyeing is done when the cloth or yarn is several shades darker than the desired finished color. It will lighten in color as it dries.

❀ Turn off the heat. Let the dye bath cool.

❀ Remove the cloth or yarn. Rinse under warm water until all the excess color has run out. Squeeze gently.

❀ Hang to dry away from direct sunlight

Get out your knitting needles and knit a hat, scarf or mittens! Or needlepoint a pillow, chair seat cover or wall hanging for your room.

Other plants to use for dyes:

Herb	Color Created
Dandelion flowers	yellow
Maple tree bark	rosy-tan
Yellow onion skins	yellow to burnt orange
Red onion skins	reddish-orange
Goldenrod flowers	yellow-brown
Elderberries	violet
Nettles	greenish-yellow

SUN BOUQUET

Capture the sun with a dried calendula bouquet! Did you know that looking at a bouquet of dried calendula flowers was once believed to give strength and comfort to the heart?

Follow the instructions for the dried yarrow flower bouquet, only use calendula flowers instead. Pick a variety of the colors—golden, yellow, orange, orangey-red—and mix together for a beautiful bouquet. Give to someone special as a surprise.

PUT SPARKLE IN YOUR EYES

A calendula eyewash eases inflamed and sore eyes. It also takes away any redness, bringing sparkle back to your eyes!

* Make calendula tea and cool.

* Fill an eyecup (get one at a drugstore) or the palm of your hand with calendula tea. Put over your eye and circle your eyes around in the tea. Be sure to keep your eye open so the tea can heal it. (This is no different from looking under-water when you are swimming or in your bathtub.) It won't sting, but soothes your eye.

* Repeat two times during the day until your eye is clear again.

Other herbs to use: echinacea (coneflower), plantain, comfrey

STORY TIME!
Mari's Gold

Once upon a time in a faraway place there lived the most generous and kind being anyone had ever known. Named Mari, she had long curly hair and wore a gown which sparkled with every color of the rainbow.

Mari was in charge of the Rainbow Makers. Whenever a large number of people gathered together to celebrate any special event, Mari directed the seven Rainbow Makers to fetch their colors and paint a beautiful rainbow in the sky. This same rainbow also created the gown she wore. The more people who were present, the larger the rainbow that was painted. When it was finished, Mari would spin a large pot of gold from her gown and place it at the end of the rainbow.

Now this was no ordinary pot of gold, for it looked different to each person who saw it. Some saw brilliant sparkly lights; others saw a city of gold or a shimmering forest. Yet all felt warm and loved inside after seeing the cauldron of gold.

After painting the rainbow, the Rainbow Makers returned to their homes. Here they kept their colors until the next time they were needed. Red was kept in the volcanoes, while orange was spun into sunrise. Yellow splashed the sun and green coated the forests. Blue was woven into the ocean, while purple webbed twilight. Last of all, midnight cradled dark blue indigo.

One day the largest celebration ever was held. The rainbow painted was so huge that its ends touched both sides of the world. Everyone was there to see it, everyone except the Grumpies, of course. The Grumpies were a grouchy people who never smiled or played. They especially didn't like the celebrations with their rainbow paintings. They would roll on the ground kicking their feet in the air and yell loudly in order to avoid seeing or hearing the happy celebrations. Happiness was definitely not one of the Grumpies' strong points.

Yet, when the largest rainbow ever to span the planet appeared, the Grumpies simply couldn't ignore it. In frustration and anger, they decided to snatch away this biggest and brightest of all rainbows once and for all.

With hollering and angry yells they came stomping into the celebration. They were just in time to watch Mari spin her pot of gold, and in the cauldron they saw a huge treasure of gold coins. Overcome with greed, the Grumpies wanted the entire pot for themselves. "We must have those coins!" they all whispered greedily. "Yes, we must, we must! We will be the richest people in all the world and at the same time we'll put a stop to all this stupid fun."

While everyone else was dancing they quietly sneaked toward the cauldron and quickly grabbed it before anyone saw them. After the pot was gone, everyone noticed that they weren't having as much fun as before. They began to complain of feeling tired and annoyed with each other, and worst of all, Mari grew weaker and weaker. Seeing that Mari was ill, everyone realized the cause of their problems. The pot of gold was gone. They knew that if Mari's pot of gold wasn't returned, she would surely die.

It was decided to send the fastest and bravest runners in the land to find Mari's pot of gold. As the people waited, Mari became sicker and sicker and began to fade until she was almost invisible. Finally, a runner returned, revealing that he had found Mari's pot of gold hidden in the camp of the Grumpies. Everyone knew it would be no easy task to reclaim Mari's gold, but soon they formed a clever plan.

Quietly and ever so softly, all Mari's people secretly crept down to the Grumpies' camp, which was on the dark, barren side of a cold mountain. When the Grumpies were all sound asleep, they suddenly burst into laughter, song and dance, doing everything they knew the Grumpies detested. They even lit fireworks and the Rainbow Makers painted a gorgeous rainbow.

Needless to say, the Grumpies were extremely surprised and upset, becoming Grumpier than ever. They were made more miserable than ever by the happy fun in their cold, lonely camp. They were so distracted by their misery that they didn't even notice when the people took Mari's pot of gold. After the pot of gold was returned to Mari, she soon grew shining and well again. With great joy everyone danced and celebrated. Then suddenly Mari hushed them while she cast a spell over the pot of gold.

Slowly the pot rose into the sky high above their heads. Then Mari shot an arrow, hitting the cauldron with a clang. The pot burst apart and all the gold showered down upon the land below. Mari proclaimed, "From now on, the gold in the pot is to turn into beautiful flowers with magical healing properties. Now everybody can see them. They will never be stolen again."

Beautiful golden-orange flowers soon rose up out of the earth. Everyone cheered for now they could see the gold anytime they wanted. Having given the best gift of all, Mari descended into the earth to nurture and care for the return of her golden flowers each spring.

Since that day, these flowers have been called Marigold in honor of Mari and her gift from the pot of gold. They are also known as calendula. Capturing the glow and brightness of the sun, these flowers still warm everyone's heart. Some say that if you peer long and deep into one of the flower's petals, you can see Mari's pot of gold.

Calendula Song

Michael Tierra

CINNAMON
Bark of Sweetness

Cinnamon is another kitchen medicine, like ginger. The cinnamon tree grows in the Orient and is used there as a spice in cooking and as a medicinal herb. Cinnamon comes from the dried inner bark of the shoots of the cinnamon tree. It has a hot energy and will warm you up nicely on cold days!

USE CINNAMON FOR:

* **feelings of coldness**
* **colds and flu with strong chills and a mild fever**
* **coughs with clear runny or white mucus**
* **vomiting, indigestion**
* **diarrhea, dysentery**
* **gas, cramps, abdominal pain**
* **whitening teeth**

Latin Name: *Cinnamomum zeylandicum, C. cassia*
Part Used: dried inner bark of the shoots of the cinnamon tree
Energy and Taste: hot energy; sweet taste
Dose for Children: Drink 1/4-1/2 cup of tea, or 1/2-1 cup milk, 2 times a day.
Make as a: tea, milk, paste, tincture, spice, powder, capsule, toothpowder, oil, potpourri, sachet, syrup, pill, candy, liniment, mulled cider, chai tea.

Cinnamon Parts

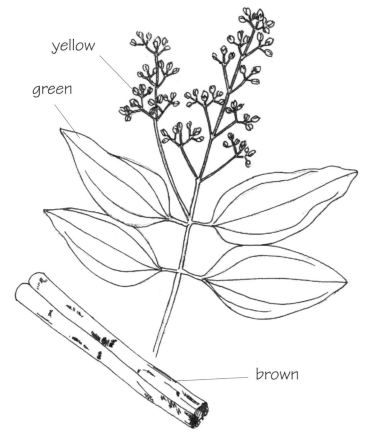

yellow

green

brown

TASTE AND FEEL

Roll a stick of cinnamon in your hands. What does it feel like? Now lick the stick. How does it taste to you? Bitter? Sweet? Mild? Spicy?

Next bite off a tiny piece of the bark and chew. How do you feel afterwards? Do you feel cooler? Warmer?

HERBAL PASTE?

No, this is not glue, but a type of medicinal candy! When herbs such as cinnamon or ginger powder are mixed with honey, they form a medicinal paste, which is called an electuary (ee-leck-chew-air-ee). This is one medicine that tastes delicious, however!

The ancient medicinal system of India (called Ayurveda—eye-your-vay-da) uses honey to make herbal pastes for many medicines. Honey is very nutritious and has a warming energy which helps clear mucus out of the body. Because it enters the bloodstream quickly, its effects are felt rapidly.

Cinnamon or ginger paste is a tasty way to stay warm all winter. It also fights off colds and flu when there are strong chills and a low fever. Cinnamon or ginger paste is especially good for relieving coughs with runny, clear-to-white mucus (do not use if there is thick yellow mucus), and easing stomachaches, gas and vomiting.

- Mix the powdered herbs with enough honey to form a paste.
- If the mixture is too gooey, add more powdered herbs. If the mixture is too dry and powdery, add a bit more honey.
- Eat in small 1/4 to 1/2 teaspoon doses two or more times a day as needed.
- To make your paste even tastier, mix it with a little clarified butter, known in India as ghee. (Ghee also has a beneficial effect on the body and helps the absorption of the herbs.)

Other Herbs to Use: ginger, fennel, garlic, slippery elm, lemon balm, chamomile.

CINNAMON BREW

Cinnamon will help you feel toasty warm inside and out. To warm up cold hands and feet, drink cinnamon tea:

- Steep 1 teaspoon cinnamon bark in hot water for 15-20 minutes. Add honey to taste and drink.

- You can also mix 1/2-1 teaspoon cinnamon powder into 1 cup hot water, add honey and drink.

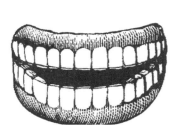

BRIGHT SMILES!

When you brush your teeth with finely ground cinnamon powder, it helps whiten and brighten your teeth. Try it! It tastes so very good. The powder must be finely ground or it can scratch your teeth.

CINNAMON MILK

Herbal milks are often used in India. Their ancient system of medicine uses these milk "decoctions" for nutrition and to heal different ailments, depending on the herbs used.

Cinnamon milk especially helps to firm loose or runny bowels. (This works well for both children and grandparents!) It also warms the body and aids digestion.

- Heat 1 cup milk in a pan to scalding.

- Add 1 teaspoon powdered cinnamon.

- Add 1 teaspoon honey, if desired and stir well.

Note: It is best to use whole milk that is also organic (free from hormones, antibiotics and other drugs). Drugs become concentrated in animal fat. Yet fat is needed to make a whole food for the body. Good quality fats are very important.

Other Herbs to Use: Try making an herbal milk with these herbs—slippery elm, fennel, ginger, licorice.

LINIMENTS

A liniment is an herbal extract that is rubbed into the skin. It treats strained muscles, bruises and arthritis. It is only for external use. Liniments keep for ten years. Store in glass jars in a cool, dark place.

☺ Powder 4 ounces of your desired herbs and put in a jar.

☺ Pour 1 pint rubbing alcohol, apple cider vinegar or olive oil over the herbs in the glass jar.

☺ Every day shake the jar for a minute to mix the herbs and liquid well. Do this for at least 2 weeks.

☺ After 2 weeks, strain the liquid: Cover a kitchen colander with some cheesecloth and place the colander in a big bowl. Pour the herbal mixture into the colander. Put on a pair of rubber gloves, then squeeze the herbs in the cheesecloth to wring out all the liquid.

☺ Pour the liquid into a glass jar and cover tightly. Toss out the herbs.

Herbs to use: cayenne, cinnamon, calendula, yarrow, comfrey, ginger.

ALL-PURPOSE LINIMENT

This formula is good for blood circulation, bruises, injuries, sore and aching muscles and arthritis. Make a liniment using the following herbs:

angelica root	1 oz.
comfrey root	1 oz.
cinnamon bark	3/4 oz.
	(or 4 drops cinnamon essential oil)
valerian root	3/4 oz.
calendula flowers	1/2 oz.
cayenne	1/4 teaspoon

CINNAMON HALVAH

Halvah is a wonderful candy made from sesame seeds and honey. Sesame seeds are very high in calcium, a mineral that strengthens your bones, teeth and nerves. Honey is warming and helps clear out mucus. When cinnamon is added, it warms you up on a blustery day and aids your digestion, too.

❀ Lightly toast 1 cup of sesame seeds in a dry skillet, stirring constantly until the seeds start popping and turn brown. Cool.

❀ Grind up the sesame seeds in a nut and seed or coffee grinder, blender or food processor until they form a paste.

❀ Mix the resulting sesame paste with 4 teaspoons cinnamon powder and 1/2 cup honey.

❀ Spread the mixture thinly on a sheet of aluminum foil and wrap it up to cover.

❀ Refrigerate for several hours.

❀ Cut into bite-sized pieces and eat.

CHAI

This delicious spicy tea is regularly drunk in India every day. It makes a great winter brew to keep you warm all season long. It is especially good for vegetarians or for people who easily feel cold. To make it less spicy, just add more milk. Chai also helps digestion, gas and colds with a lot of chills.

ↄ Combine together in a pot:

    1 tablespoon grated fresh ginger or 1/4 teaspoon ginger powder
    7 peppercorns
    1 cinnamon stick
    5 cloves
    15 cardamom seeds
    1 peel from a whole orange (dry or fresh)
    1 pint water

ↄ Cover the pot and simmer 10 minutes.

ↄ Add 1/2 cup milk and simmer covered another 10 minutes.

ↄ Strain and sweeten with honey.

ↄ Adults may brew this with black tea if they wish. That is how it is traditionally made in India.

MULLED CIDER

Imagine playing or reading by a crackling fire on a cold winter's night. Wouldn't a mug of mulled apple-cinnamon cider be a perfect addition? It certainly would warm your insides up for the night.
Mulled cider has been enjoyed throughout much of Europe during the winter months. It is especially enjoyed on festive occasions—winter parties after ice skating or sledding, Christmas parties after caroling, New Year's Eve and during other celebrations.

You may not realize it, but you probably have all the ingredients for mulled apple-cinnamon cider in your own kitchen right now! If not, they are easily purchased at a grocery store.

- Mix together 2 cinnamon sticks broken into pieces, 1 whole clove, 2 teaspoons chopped and dried orange peel and 1/2 teaspoon allspice.

- Stir into 2 cups apple juice or cider.

- Heat and simmer covered for 20 minutes.

- Cool to drinking temperature.

- Strain. Pour into mugs and add a whole cinnamon stick to each mug.

"ZIPPITY-DO-DA" PASTE

This spicy herbal "candy" helps relieve colds, coughs with chills, sore throats and clear-to-white runny mucus in the head or lungs: Mix 1/2 teaspoon each of powdered ginger, black pepper and 1 teaspoon anise seeds. Blend in honey to form a paste. This is a traditional mixture used in India. It is called Trikatu (Trih-ka-too) there. Eat in 1/4-1/2 teaspoon doses two or more times a day as needed.

DID YOU KNOW . . .

☞ Chinese cinnamon, called *Cinnamomum cassia*, is even stronger in taste and warming effects than the common cinnamon we find in grocery stores. It helps eliminate low back pain and weak, cold legs made worse or caused by coldness and damp weather.

☞ The Chinese also frequently use the twigs of this species of cinnamon tree for colds, flu, slight fever, abundant chills and lung congestion with clear to white mucus.

ANT BARRIER!

Did you know that ants do not like cinnamon? To keep them off your counters and out of your plants, sprinkle cinnamon powder along their tracks and around the areas they are traveling. They won't cross the cinnamon barrier. Soon, they will leave the area entirely.

STORY TIME!
Cinnamon, Queen of the Spices

A long time ago all the spices gathered together in a big meeting. There was turmeric in her brilliant orange-yellow gown, ginger in his golden-papery robe, hard-shelled nutmeg, sweet star-shaped anise, chili wrapped in fire engine red, and many more—cumin, coriander, fennel, dill, black pepper, caraway, mustard.

When the spices tried to start their meeting, none would stop talking. Spice after spice flared up, arguing over who would be leader. Their sharp chattering rose to a thunderous roar until it was unbearable.

Mustard seed, so tiny she could barely be seen or heard, had an idea. She hopped up and down as fast as she could until the entire spice circle seemed showered by the yellow popping seed. Finally all was silent and mustard told her idea. "Let us each put a tiny bit of ourselves into the magic cauldron and create a new spice to be our leader. That way we will all be a part of the leader."

The spices liked that idea. One by one they put a pinch of themselves into the magic cauldron, each adding its own special flavor. When the last spice had been added, all the spices focused on the magic cauldron in their center.

Slowly the cauldron began shaking and rumbling, bubbling and vibrating. Then the cauldron started spinning. Faster and faster it whirled until the pot cracked. Thick roots suddenly thrust out of the cracks into the earth. Then a strong tree shot six feet into the air and burst into tiny yellow flowers.

In a sweet, melodic voice the tree said, "Thank you, dear spices, for your wonderful gift. From now on, let it be known in all the lands that I am Cinnamon, Queen of the Spices."

Soon cinnamon became one of the favorite spices eaten throughout the world. It is used both as a spice in cooking, and as an herb or healing medicine. As the "Queen of Spices," she bestows her sweet, warm, strengthening powers on all who use her. Now when the spices gather at their meetings, which would normally be heated events, Queen Cinnamon keeps order and peace among all the other spices.

DANDELION
Weed That Strengthens

Dandelion, one of our most common plants, grows everywhere across the United States and much of Europe. Herbalists in Europe, China and India have used dandelion for centuries, and still do. It has been widely respected by people for its healing powers for hundreds of years. Perhaps that's why it seems to grow everywhere.

Unfortunately, many people regard dandelion as a pesty weed today. If people knew even some of its many healing powers, they would not be so quick to dig it out of their yards and gardens!

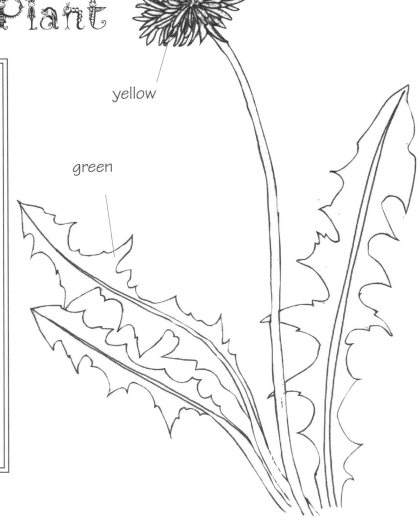

yellow

green

USE DANDELION FOR:

* skin problems and eruptions such as measles, chicken pox, eczema
* indigestion
* stomachache
* constipation
* anemia
* blood purification
* acne
* hepatitis

Latin Name: *Taraxacum officinalis*
Parts Used: leaves and roots
Energy and Taste: cold energy; bitter but pleasant taste
Dose for Children: Drink 1/2 to 1 cup dandelion tea 2 times a day.
Make as a: tea, capsule, potherb, sun tea, tincture, wash, bitters, powder, pill, dye.

DANDELION CLEANSING POTION

Drinking dandelion tea helps cleanse the blood and clear up eczema, rashes, chicken-pox and measles. It also helps your digestion and makes your bowels move, thus preventing constipation.

* Dry chopped dandelion root or purchase some from the store. (If you find roasted dandelion at the store, skip the next step.)

* Put some of the dried dandelion root in a pan on medium heat and stir frequently until the root becomes a deep brownish color.

* Add 1-2 teaspoons of roasted dandelion root to 1 cup of boiling water. (The more herb you put in, the stronger the taste.)

* Simmer covered for 15 minutes.

* Strain, add honey to taste, and drink.

DANDELION "COFFEE"

This strong tea is loved throughout most of Europe. The peasants of France, Germany and Italy all drink a daily cup of this tea.

Dandelion "coffee" clears heat and purifies the blood and liver. This is exactly opposite to what regular coffee does. (Coffee puts heat and toxins into the liver.) When the liver is cleared of heat and toxins, people feel better, more relaxed & less irritable and angry. Often people who get too angry at the pretty dandelions growing in their lawns are the very ones who need them! To make a delicious dandelion coffee:

* Simmer 2 teaspoons roasted dandelion root and 1 teaspoon roasted chicory root in 2 cups boiling water.

* Make a tea as above. Add honey to taste.

SECRET CLEAR SKIN BREW

If you have acne, the quickest way to clear your skin is to drink 2 cups of dandelion "coffee" every day. For more lasting results, also stop eating sweets and fats. You'll be amazed at how rapidly even the most broken-out skin will clear up beautifully.

SWEET BITTERS!

itters is a drink made of bitter-tasting herbs. A teaspoon of bitters is taken before each meal to stimulate digestive juices, such as hydrochloric acid and bile. This in turn stimulates appetite and even helps bowel elimination. Bitters keep 1 to 3 years. Store in dark glass bottles in a cool dark place. Before eating, take 1/2-1 teaspoon of the bitters.

To make, follow the directions for making a glycerite in the section on echinacea (coneflower). Use dandelion leaf and root, chamomile, fennel seed and the peel of a whole fresh or dried orange or tangerine.

DANDELION GARLAND

Make a pretty chain of dandelion flowers and wear it in your hair. Or give it to a good friend or your mother to wear.

* Pick about a dozen dandelions from the base of their stems.

* Cut a tiny slit in the middle of each dandelion stem. Be sure to make it very small, otherwise the dandelions will slide through the slit when you make the garland.

* Holding one dandelion, slide the stem of a second dandelion through the slit of the first until it stops at the flower head.

* Take a third dandelion and slide it through the slit of the second dandelion. Continue until all the dandelions have been added. Now you have a dandelion chain.

* To form the garland, slide the stem of the first dandelion into the slit of the last one on the chain. Weave any loose stems in among the others to finish off the garland.

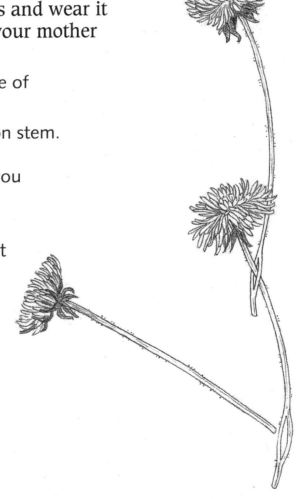

POTHERB

A potherb is any plant whose leaves are cooked and eaten. Some are steamed, others are fried in olive oil or added uncooked to beans or soups. Many greens may be eaten as a pot herb— dandelion, fennel, lambs quarters, sorrel, malvae, nettle and purslane are just a few examples.

DANDELION POTHERB

Young spring dandelion leaves are loaded with minerals, such as potassium and iron, which are wonderful for your blood and nerves. They also contain a lot of vitamins. In fact, dandelion greens contain 7,000 units of Vitamin A in each ounce. That's a lot! Vitamin A is very good for your skin and improves your eyesight.

One way to enjoy dandelion leaves is as a potherb. Eating dandelion salad greens in the springtime is a great way to cleanse your body after winter. This can then help prevent those nasty spring colds. The younger green leaves have the best flavor and are less bitter.

※ Place several young dandelion leaves (about 20 leaves per person) in a steamer basket and set in a pot of water on the stove.

※ Turn on the heat and cook for 5-10 minutes, until the leaves are wilted. Remove the leaves from the pot and place in a bowl.

※ Season as desired—lemon juice and pepper are good. Add some olive oil or butter, too. The oil is needed to help the body absorb the dandelion's minerals, and lemon juice makes the iron in greens more available to the body.

※ Alternatively, stir-fry the leaves in a little olive oil and garlic.

WISH UPON AN HERB

When the yellow dandelion flowers go to seed, they make cottony puffs that scatter with the wind. Pick one of these puffs and hold it in your hand. Then close your eyes and make a wish with all your heart and mind. Now open your eyes, take a deep breath and blow as hard as you can, thinking of your wish. If all the parachute-like seeds blow away, your wish will come true. If some remain, only part of your wish may be realized.

DID YOU KNOW . . .
A long time ago, children would wish upon a dandelion seed. They would try to blow off all the seeds from a single stem in one breath. If they did it, then they believed their wish would come true. Other children would count how many puffs it took to blow off the seeds and recite: "Count how many blows it takes till your true love becomes your mate."

PICKING HERBS

ave you ever wondered if there is a proper way to pick plants? Here are a few guidelines for picking plants with respect. This helps them grow better:

- First, it is a good idea to give thanks for the plant's life. Then ask the plant if it's all right to pick it. Wait a moment, and if you hear a "yes" inside yourself, then go ahead and pick some of the plant. If you hear a "no" inside yourself, then don't pick the plant.

- Some people leave an offering of thanks when they pick herbs. This is a gift in return for the plant's life and healing ability. It should be something special, like a song, a strand of your hair, even a penny. It is not the offering so much as the thankfulness in your heart that matters.

- When picking plants, it is very important that you don't take every one you see. Pick through them, as if you were weeding or thinning a garden, leaving about 1/3 of everything you see to reseed and grow back year after year.

- Pick plants away from roads (at least fifteen feet), as those near roads can absorb the lead from car exhaust. It is also best not to pick herbs in areas which have recently been sprayed with poisonous chemicals.

STORY TIME!
The Lion and the Wise Teacher

There once lived a wise teacher who had snow-white hair and a long white beard. His best friend was a lion with a golden curly mane. Daily the teacher shared his knowledge with people who came for his advice. As he taught them, the lion rested by his feet and basked in the wise man's love.

One day a terrible illness struck the country, making many people and animals sick. The lion fell ill with the disease and was in great pain day and night. The wise teacher tried all of his remedies and knowledge, but nothing helped. The lion was dying and the teacher felt tremendous grief.

In another part of the land a cruel magician discovered a cure for the strange disease, but didn't want to share it with anyone. When he heard about the sick lion he had an idea. Traveling to the wise teacher, he offered to heal his lion-friend. Joyfully the teacher accepted and offered to reward the magician with whatever he wished.

The magician said gleefully, "I agree to heal the lion. In return I ask that you give up your life." He believed that after he healed the lion and the wise man was gone, he'd be the most famous person in the land. The teacher was very sad about this offer, but he cared more for the lion than for himself, so he agreed.

The magician pulled several dark roots of a secret plant out of his bag. He cooked a tea from them and made the lion drink lots of the tea for several days. Soon the lion was well again. Returning to the teacher, the magician claimed the wise man's life. With one last loving look at his dear friend, the lion, the magician replied, "I am yours."

With that, the magician mumbled some odd words and waved his hands in a strange pattern. The teacher fell to the ground. "Ah-ha!" shouted the magician in triumph. "Now I will be rich and famous."

When the cured lion heard the magician yell those awful words of triumph, he leapt upon the magician and completely swallowed him up. Then in great sadness, the lion lay down by the teacher and went into a very deep sleep.

When the Sun and Earth saw what happened, they decided to do something special. The Earth shook in great waves, making both the lion's and the teacher's bodies tremble and shift until they became a part of the Earth. Then the Sun shone on them until seeds sprouted into tall and beautiful plants.

The plant had strong medicine. Its flowers were large and golden like the lion's mane, and its leaves were jagged and shaped like the lion's teeth. After the plant's golden petals faded and died, the seeds sprouted into silky white puffs in honor of the wise teacher and his snow-white hair. Then the breeze carried the seeds to other lands to grow. In this way, the teacher and the lion were still able to help heal people of their diseases.

Today this plant is called Dandelion, or Lion's Tooth. It is easily found and is used to heal many illnesses. Next time you see a dandelion, look for the lion and the wise man in its flowers and leaves, for they are still there.

Dandelion Song

Michael Tierra

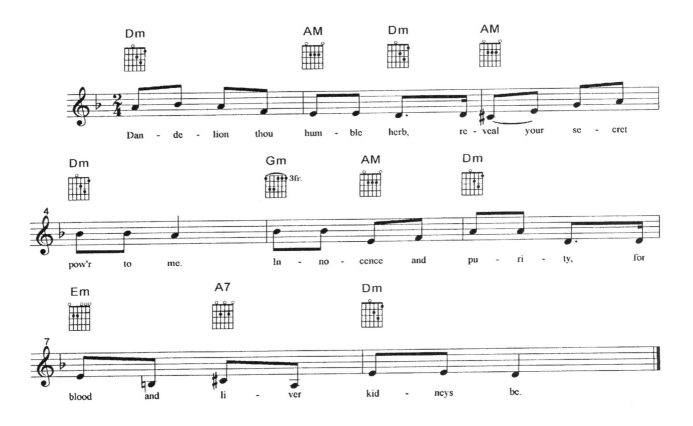

Dan - de - lion thou hum - ble herb, re - veal your se - cret
pow'r to me. In - no - cence and pu - ri - ty, for
blood and li - ver kid - neys be.

YARROW
The Wound Herb

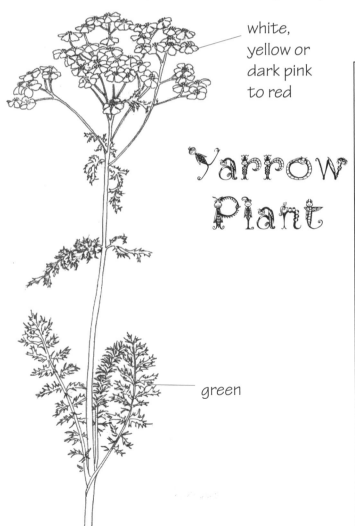

Yarrow has been used all over the world for thousands of years. The ancient Greek hero, Achilles, is said to have used yarrow to help stop his soldiers' wounds from bleeding. In fact, the Latin name of this herb, *Achilles millefolium*, is taken from "Achilles" for this very reason. The species name, *millefolium*, means "thousand leaves" because of its thousands of feathery little leaflets.

Yarrow flowers are either yellow, white or dark pink to red in color. The white yarrow flower is used for medicine, while the yellow and pink yarrow are used as ornamental flowers. (That means they are pretty to look at!)

white, yellow or dark pink to red

green

USE YARROW FOR:

* internal bleeding
* wounds, cuts
* coughs
* colds, flu
* fever
* burns
* bruises
* toothaches
* measles, boils
* infections
* nosebleeds
* upset stomach

Latin Name: *Achilles millefolium*
Part Used: the above-ground portion (stem, leaves, flowers)
Energy and Tastes: neutral energy; bitter and sour tastes
Dose for Children: Drink 1/4-1/2 cup yarrow tea every hour until the symptoms are gone.
Make as a: tea, tincture, salve, wash, capsule, powder, bitters, fomentation, poultice, oil, foot bath, bath, liniment, mouthwash, dream pillow, dried bouquet.

GET WELL FAST POTION

Yarrow causes the body to sweat, making it very useful for fevers, colds and flu. For best results, make a strong tea using 1/2 teaspoon each of yarrow, elder, chamomile and lemon balm and 1/4 teaspoon each of ginger and licorice to 1 cup water. Add some honey to taste, and drink in 1/4-1/2 cup doses throughout the day to quickly chase your cold away!

YARROW ORNAMENTAL BOUQUET

Yarrow flowers dry well and make a beautiful dried flower bouquet. Combine all three colors or just two, if you wish. Any combination will be pretty.

- Cut a bunch of yarrow stalks and flowers. Cut them at their bases near the ground.

- Using a long string, tie the stalks together at their bottoms.

- Tack the end of the string to the ceiling, a beam, top of a wall or a picture hook out of the sunlight.

- Hang until dry, which is usually about two weeks.

- Arrange them in a vase without water. They keep a long time.

YARROW PICK-UP STICKS

To make:

* Cut two dozen yarrow stems with flowers and dry (see Yarrow Ornamental Bouquet).

* Cut off the flower heads and use them in a flower arrangement.

* Use the dried stems for Pick-Up Sticks.

STOP-BLEEDING BALM

ne of the reasons yarrow is very healing for wounds is because it does stop bleeding. For this the herb is applied directly to the wound as a poultice (see plantain for making poultices). Just "bruise" the fresh leaves, then press them into the wound and bandage in place. If you have powdered yarrow on hand you can sprinkle that on the wound to stop any bleeding, too.

DID YOU KNOW . . .

In ancient China, yarrow stalks were once used to help tell the future and answer questions. The Chinese would toss the yarrow stalks into the air and then "read" the pattern the stalks made after they fell to the ground. This is called "divination," and the book the Chinese used for answers is called the *I Ching*. Yarrow stalks were perfect for this because they are quite stiff, and yet light. Today we can use the same stalks for pick-up-sticks.

OH NO! MEASLES AND CHICKENPOX!

Yarrow can help measles and chicken-pox eruptions to appear faster and so heal quicker. For this to work, take 2 "0" yarrow capsules at the first signs of measles or chickenpox. Continue taking every 3 hours for 1-2 days.

NATIVE AMERICANS USED YARROW, TOO

The Native Americans used yarrow for wounds. They also chewed yarrow to soothe toothaches, and drank its tea for stomachaches. To treat nosebleeds they would roll up leaves and insert them into their nostrils to stop the bleeding. (Don't try this by yourself!)

CAPSULES

 apsules are made from gelatin and filled with powdered herbs. They are best used with herbs which are bitter tasting or are strong acting. Milder-tasting herbs, such as licorice or lemon balm, are better as teas. Yarrow, coneflower (echinacea), dandelion, cayenne and ginger are examples of strong-tasting herbs that can be taken in capsule form.

Capsules come in several sizes. The most common are the small "0" sized cap and the larger "00" sized cap. The "0" capsule is best for children as it is small and easily swallowed. Usually the dose for children is to take one "0" capsule 1-3 times a day. One ounce of herbs fills about 60 "0" caps or 30 "00" caps.

- Powder the herbs you want to encapsulate, or purchase the herbs already powdered.

- Pour the powder into a bowl.

- Separate the 2 parts of the capsule. Holding the larger side, tap its open end down into the powder until it is full.

- Put the two parts of the capsule back together and place into a clean bowl.

- Continue until all the powder or capsules are gone.

- Store the capsules in a tightly sealed jar in a cool dark place.

STORY TIME!
Ta'ro, The Shining Star

There once lived a tiny but bright star named Ta'ro. As the youngest star in a huge family, she always did what she wanted. When the star family decided to shine brightly, Ta'ro blinked off and on like a turn signal. When the stars formed a pretty pattern, Ta'ro played tag.

One night when all the stars showed their dark sides and hid, Ta'ro swelled up until hundreds of brilliant points shot out from her round belly. This was too much for the grumbling star family. Ta'ro decided she'd better leave, so she skipped across the heavens to visit some of her distant relatives.

At first she was welcome, but there, too, Ta'ro was mischievous. When her cousins turned a soft blue, Ta'ro shone a fiery red. When the others shimmered in the sky, Ta'ro faded until she looked like a dull and dirty coin. And when the elder stars took turns at showing their twinkling faces in the night sky, Ta'ro changed her shape from a circle to a triangle or a square. This annoyed all the surrounding stars so much that Ta'ro had to slip quickly away again.

Flying through the sky, Ta'ro soon found a new place. It was a beautiful blue planet hugged by white swirling clouds, called Earth. At first everything seemed fine as Ta'ro was on her best behavior and Earth's stars welcomed her in their midst. Yet after a bit, Ta'ro was up to her old tricks, and started skipping about the night sky changing her shape, playing hide and seek, or trying on different colors as before.

Soon, Earth's stars became quite upset with Ta'ro. Feeling very hurt and sad, Ta'ro's light dimmed until she could barely be seen. She thought she had tried to fit in with the stars wherever she went. Yet, she never managed to do so. She always ended up in trouble because of her mischief-making.

In her sadness Ta'ro grew duller and duller until she was barely a speck of light in the night sky. Suddenly Ta'ro knew she'd never fit into any other star's plans or purposes. Instead, she had to follow her own heart and shine as only she could do. A plan began to form in her mind and Ta'ro shone a little brighter as she thought about it.

One black night when the sun was showing his back and darkening the Earth, Ta'ro was ready. She started spinning faster and faster until suddenly she became a shooting star and zoomed across the night sky in a brilliant display of light. Down, down, down she fell until she landed on Earth.

Slowly, Ta'ro began to change. Roots grew out of her bottom points, burrowing into the dirt. Her body stretched up tall and thin toward the night sky. Several points spread out sideways into soft green feathery leaves. The remaining points at her head burst into dozens of tiny flowers.

Finally, Ta'ro felt like her very own self. She switched her colors from white to yellow or red as she pleased. Other times she shifted with the seasons, sometimes peeking slightly above ground, other times growing tall and strong. In winter she showed her dark side and disappeared altogether.

What Ta'ro liked most was that she did not have to hide her inner light and joy any longer. Instead, she had made herself into a powerful healing plant-medicine for those who lived on Earth.

One day, when someone was picking some of her flowers she spoke her star name, Ta'ro. The person thought she had heard the word "yarrow," and so she has been called since that time. Ta'ro doesn't mind, for now she is free to be her true self, and has found a way to be welcomed and accepted as she is, rather than as others want her to be.

DREAM PILLOW

For hundreds of years people have put aromatic (fragrant) herbs under their pillows at night to help them sleep. Soon they discovered that many herbs helped them remember their dreams as well. If you would like to remember your dreams better, then you can make a dream pillow.

A dream pillow is a pouch of dried herbs placed under the pillow or by the nose to invite dreams while sleeping.

- Put the herbs in a small sack, pouch or bag. Be sure to tie or sew the open end closed. You can also make your own bag. A good size is 6" x 8".

- Place the bag under your pillow or by your nose at night.

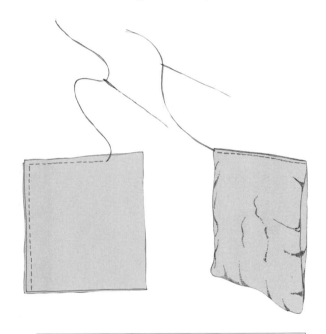

Herbs to use: yarrow, lemon balm, rose petals, lavender, chamomile. The herbs hops and mugwort are good, too. (Even though yarrow is not a strong-smelling herb, it has traditionally been used in dream pillows, so it can be added, too.)

WHO WILL MY SWEETHEART BE?

In olden times yarrow was used as a dream pillow to bring a vision of a future husband or wife. If you want to try this, too, place a yarrow dream pillow or the fresh plant under your pillow before going to sleep and repeat the following:

*"Thou pretty herbs of Venus' tree,
Thy true name, it is yarrow;
Now who will my best friend be,
Pray tell me to-morrow."*

HERBS TO THE RESCUE!
A Quick Guide to Treating Illnesses

When you get the sniffles, a sore throat or a stomach-ache, how do you know which herbs to use? That's a very good question, and there are several answers.

First, as you learn about herbs, you'll begin to remember for what each herb is used. We learned about several herbs and their uses in Chapter 2.

Then you can have on hand a set of herbal preparations already made just for different symptoms. This is called a first aid kit.

Next, you can look up your symptom, such as a headache or a cold, in books and see which herbs are best used for that symptom. In this chapter there is a simple list of children's symptoms and the herbs to choose for each symptom.

HERBAL FIRST AID KIT

Y ou can create your very own first aid kit very easily. If you made all the herbal preparations for the herbs in Chapter 2, then you have already created your own kit. And you didn't even know it!

A first aid kit is a group of various herbal preparations such as a salve, tincture, oil, capsule and so on. They are used for various minor health problems like cuts, insect bites, coughs, colds or upset stomachs. Normally a first aid kit is kept at home in a medicine chest. But, it can also be taken in the car or on trips. Store your remedies together in a decorated shoe box, old lunch box or cloth bag. You could even sew a special bag yourself. Herbal first aid kits make great gifts for friends and family.

It's important that you label and date each herbal preparation. Then you know what it is and how old it is. The tinctures, oils and salves keep many years. Syrups, capsules, pills, pastes, powders and bulk herbs lose their potency quickly, so they should be replaced every six months.

It's a good idea to list the ingredients of each preparation on its label. You can also add what it is used for and how to take it. Then in an emergency you have all the information you need right at your fingertips.

Other items that may be included in your kit are alcohol wipes, an eye cup, gauze, adhesive tape, bandages, needle and thread, small scissors, tweezers and empty gelatin capsules. Add whatever else you think might fit your needs.

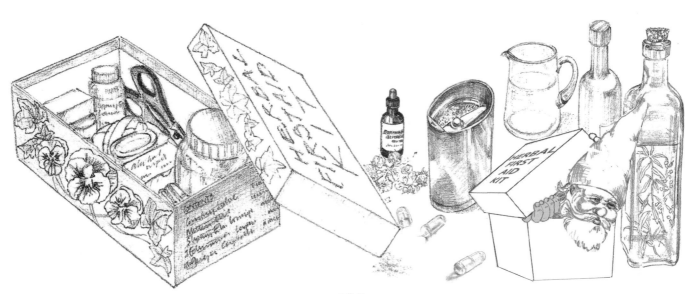

Remedies	Possible Herbs	Uses	How to Take
Bitters	dandelion, yarrow, chamomile, citrus peel, ginger	weak digestion, poor appetite, indigestion	Use 1/2-1 tsp. before or after meals.
Cayenne capsules, powder	cayenne powder	external bleeding, colds, flu, coldness (to warm up), low energy, poor digestion, cramps	To stop bleeding, sprinkle on the wound and take 2 "0" caps internally. Take one "0" cap with water for other symptoms.
Chamomile tea, bath, wash, fomentation, mouthwash	dried chamomile flowers	indigestion, restless sleep, crying, whining, skin problems, teething	Use 1/4-1/2 cup doses 2-3 times/day. Use other methods as needed.
Cinnamon capsules, milk, tea, powder	cinnamon	coldness, coughs with clear or white runny mucus, vomiting, diarrhea or indigestion due to coldness, toothpowder	Milk: 1 tsp. to 1 c. milk or 1/2-1 tsp. powder to 1 cup water; drink 1/2-1 cup milk; drink 1/4-1/2 cup tea; 1 "0" capsule with water; add honey to form a paste and take in 1/4 tsp. doses.
Dream Pillow	yarrow, chamomile, lemon balm	sleeping aid	Put near your nose while you sleep.
Ear oil	mullein, calendula, echinacea, garlic	earaches	Put 2-3 drops in your ear several times a day.

Remedies	Possible Herbs	Uses	How to Take
Elder Oil	elder, calendula, chamomile	burns, cuts, sores, abrasions, chapped skin	Apply directly to the hurt skin area as needed.
Elder Syrup	elder, yarrow, lemon balm, ginger, garlic	colds, flu, lung or sinus congestion	Use 1/2-1 tsp. every 2-3 hours.
Foot Powder	powdered slippery elm or calendula	bad foot odor, sore or itching feet	Sprinkle on your feet and toes, morning and night.
Gargle tea	echinacea, licorice, ginger, elder, calendula, a pinch of cayenne	sore throats	Gargle with 1/2 cup tea 3 times a day or as needed.
Garlic bulb juice, cider, plaster, syrup, "sandwiches"	fresh garlic	colds, flu, fever, coughs, strong chills, bronchitis, sore throat, worms, earache	Use 1/3-1 raw clove in oil, 1-3 times daily; 1/2 tsp. syrup every 1-2 hours; 1/4-1/2 tsp. juice every 2 hours; plaster as needed.
Ginger capsule, tea, bath, wash, gargle	ginger, fresh or powdered	sore throat, colds, flu, chills, cramps, coldness, nausea, stomachache, white to clear runny mucus	Use 1/4-1/2 cup tea every 2-3 hours; one "0" capsule 3 times daily; gargle 3 times daily; bath and wash as needed.
Lemon balm bath, tea, mouthwash	dried lemon balm leaves	fever, colds, flu, cough, nervousness, whining, crying	Use 1/2-1 cup tea every 2 hours; bath and mouthwash as needed.

Remedies	Possible Herbs	Uses	How to Take
Liniment	cinnamon, cayenne, comfrey, calendula	injuries, bruises, sore aching muscles and joints	Apply as needed.
Mouthwash tea	echinacea, yarrow, lemon balm, ginger, chamomile, a pinch of cayenne	gum and mouth infections	Swish around your mouth 3-4 times daily.
Oil	ginger, comfrey, calendula, plantain, yarrow, elder, echinacea, cayenne	sore aching muscles, cuts, bites, stings, wounds, bruises, burns	Apply frequently throughout the day until the problem is gone.
Paste	ginger, black pepper, anise seeds	colds and coughs with chills, sore throats and clear or white runny mucus	Use 1/4-1/2 tsp. every 2-3 hours.
Pills	powdered slippery elm and licorice with honey	sore and hoarse throats, coughs	Use 1-2 pills every 2-3 hours.
Plantain	dried plantain leaves	use as a wash or poultice for poison oak or ivy	Use daily until the problem has gone away.
Salve	comfrey, plantain, calendula, echinacea, yarrow	skin irritations, cuts, wounds, bruises, bites, stings, burns, sores, eruptions, itching	Rub on 3-4 times daily until the problem is gone.

Remedies	Possible Herbs	Uses	How to Take
Slippery elm powder, lozenge, pills, porridge	slippery elm powder	nausea, vomiting, nutrition, skin irritation	Use 1-2 pills or lozenges every 2-3 hours; 1 bowl porridge as needed; powder on skin as needed.
Syrup	licorice, mullein, ginger, lemon balm, plantain, elder, fennel, garlic	Coughs, mucus, congestion, bronchitis, asthma	Use 1/2-1 tsp. every 2-3 hours.
Tincture/ Glycerite	echinacea	infections, inflammations, bites, stings, fevers, colds, flu	Use 15-30 drops every 2 hours; two "0" caps every 2 hours.
Toothpowder	powdered fennel with baking powder	Cleaning teeth and gums	Use as needed.
Yarrow	yarrow powder	Bleeding	Sprinkle on the wound as needed until bleeding stops; take 2 "0" capsules internally.

KITCHEN MEDICINES

Did you know that your kitchen is a big medicine chest? Most all spices used in cooking are also used for healing in many countries. Also, there are many foods that have healing power as well. The next time you get a cold, cough or tummy-ache, look no further than your kitchen cupboards!

CULINARY HERBS

Culinary herbs are herbs used in cooking. They flavor food so it tastes good. Many culinary herbs also help digestion. There are lots of kitchen herbs that are easily grown. Some are garlic, cayenne, basil, parsley, fennel, sage, rosemary, thyme, oregano, dill, coriander and cilantro.

SPICES HEAL, TOO!

Did you know that kitchen spices also have healing powers? To use them, make a tea, simmer with milk or take as a paste with honey. We already talked about ginger, garlic, cinnamon, fennel and cayenne. Here are a few more healing spices and their medicinal uses:

Anise: colic, gas, coughs

Basil: fevers, colds, flu, headache, indigestion, cramps, nausea, vomiting, constipation

Bay: gas, indigestion, as a poultice over the chest for bronchitis and coughs

Black pepper: coughs with white mucus, sore throat; at the first sign of a cold take with honey

Caraway: indigestion, gas, colic, nervous conditions

Cardamom: indigestion, gas

Cloves: gas, vomiting, nausea, indigestion, blood circulation; the oil of cloves can be rubbed on the gums for toothache. (If you don't have the oil, simply chew the cloves.)

Coriander: gas, indigestion, fevers

Cumin: gas, indigestion

Marjoram: upset stomach, headache, colic, nausea, seasickness, nervous complaints, abdominal cramps; oil of marjoram can be rubbed onto the gums to relieve toothaches

Mustard seed: stimulates the circulation; as a plaster for lung congestion, aches, sprains, spasms

Rosemary: headaches, gas, indigestion, colic, nausea, fevers; as a hair rinse after shampoo

Sage: early stages of colds and flu, sinus congestion, stops sweating, diarrhea, bladder infections; use as a gargle for sore throats and ulcerations in the mouth

Thyme: acute bronchitis, whooping cough, laryngitis, intestinal worms, indigestion, diarrhea, lack of appetite, mouthwash; use as a cleansing wash, tincture or oil on the skin for fungus, scabies and lice

Turmeric: constipation, fevers, nose bleed, wounds

Note: Spices found in supermarket spice sections are not generally very strong medicines because of the spice processing techniques. Purchase your spices and herbs at a health food or herb store. You can also mail-order them from suppliers listed in Resources at the back of this book.

DON'T THROW THOSE PEELS AWAY!

Whenever you eat an orange, tangerine or grapefruit, or use a lemon, don't throw away the peels. The peels of lemons, oranges, tangerines and grapefruits are very healing. The Chinese use fruit peels, especially tangerine peels, in many of their herbal formulas to help circulate the herbs throughout the body.

Set the peels on a counter or tray in a dry, warm place out of the sunlight. They should be dry within a few days. Store in glass jars with lids. Then when you need them, make a tea by simmering covered 2 large slices of peel in 1 cup water for 10 minutes. **It is best to use organic fruit which hasn't been sprayed with chemicals.**

☺ Orange and tangerine peel tea has a wonderful citrus-like flavor. It is a great aid to digestion, helping to alleviate gas, nausea and vomiting. It also clears white to clear-colored mucus.

☺ Lemon peels are made into a tea in Italy and drunk after meals to help digestion.

☺ Grapefruit peel tea lowers fevers and treats colds and flu.

COLD AND FLU CONGEE

Do you lose your appetite whenever you have a cold or flu? Most people do. Here is a very light food you can eat to maintain your strength while you are sick. It is easy to digest and helps heal colds and flu with chills and a slight fever.

🦎 Simmer 1/2 cup rice in 2 cups water for about 2-3 hours until it reaches a porridge-like consistency.

🦎 While still hot, add 3 chopped scallions or garlic cloves and 6 slices of fresh ginger.

🦎 Bring the entire mixture to a boil, cover and simmer for 5 minutes.

🦎 Eat 2 bowls a day on an empty stomach. It should cause a light sweat, improving your condition.

SESAME SALT/GOMASIO

This is a tasty seasoning for foods and is also a tonic for the heart and body. One teaspoon of this salt can be taken nightly by people suffering from heart weakness. It is also beneficial for heartburn and headache when taken as these occur. For those who feel cold, weak or tired, a sprinkling of gomasio (go-_ma_-sea-oh) on your food every day will help strengthen your body.

Sesame salt does not create thirst as the oil from the sesame seeds coats the salt. This helps the salt directly enter the cells of the body. It is delicious sprinkled on your food as a salt substitute. To make:

✳ Roast 1 teaspoon sea salt in a pan until a faint odor of chlorine rises from salt.

✳ Next roast 7 tablespoons sesame seeds in a pan, stirring continuously until they have popped, about 10 minutes.

✳ Combine the salt and seeds in a nut and seed or coffee grinder, blender or food processor and grind just until most of the seeds have been crushed. If you grind it too long, it will turn into "butter." The best gomasio by far is made by hand using a ridged mortar and pestle, known in Japan as a surabachi.

THYME FOR ALL SEASONS

Variations of gomasio are made in other countries. The Arabs eat a mixture of thyme and coriander seeds mixed with gomasio. They eat this with olive oil on bread. It can be taken on a daily basis to help heal coughs and prevent fevers, colds and parasites.

❧ Powder 1 teaspoon dried thyme with 1 tablespoon gomasio (and 1/4 teaspoon coriander seeds, if desired) in a nut and seed or coffee grinder, blender or food processor.

❧ Eat on bread dipped in olive oil.

❧ People in Israel combine sesame seeds and salt with hyssop for a similar seasoning. Try it, or create your own gomasio combinations!

SPICY BATH

This bath creates a sweat, which helps relieve fever, chills, colds and flu and stimulates the circulation.

▦ Combine 1 teaspoon each powdered turmeric and ginger and 1/4 teaspoon cayenne pepper.

▦ Put in a hot tub of bath water.

▦ Stay in the tub for 20 minutes, then dry off, dress warmly and get under several layers of covers. You will soon start sweating, which will break the fever and heal the cold or flu. Stay under the covers for 20-30 minutes, then change into dry clothes.

A PLUM IN YOUR NAVEL?

There is a special Japanese plum that is very healing. Called umeboshi (oo-me-bow-she), it is pickled in salt. Umeboshi plums can be found in oriental groceries or health food stores, either in the form of whole plums or as a paste. They are very sour and salty.

When a whole umeboshi plum is taped to the navel it stops motion sickness! The plum or paste can also be eaten to help digestion, certain types of headaches, nausea, tummy aches and cramps, migraines and acidity. Keep a small jar of umeboshi paste in your car. Then the next time you feel car sick, eat a little of it.

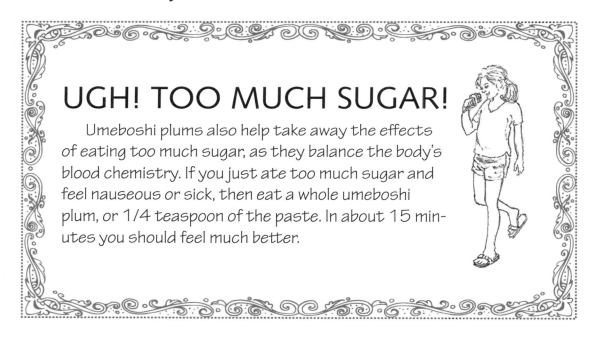

UGH! TOO MUCH SUGAR!

Umeboshi plums also help take away the effects of eating too much sugar, as they balance the body's blood chemistry. If you just ate too much sugar and feel nauseous or sick, then eat a whole umeboshi plum, or 1/4 teaspoon of the paste. In about 15 minutes you should feel much better.

RAW BROWN RICE

The native people who live in the Himalayas of India and Tibet eat a little raw brown rice every day before breakfast (on an empty stomach) to prevent parasites. If you are traveling to other countries, or need to remove intestinal parasites, slowly chew a teaspoonful or two of raw brown rice first thing each morning for a week or two.

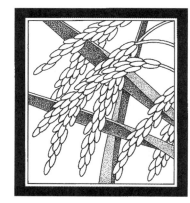

HERBAL "SWEETENERS"

se herbs to flavor your food and drinks instead of sugar! Not only are they healthier for your body, but they add interesting flavors, too. Try: anise, fennel, licorice or cinnamon.

One herb that grows in South America, **stevia**, is a natural substitute for sugar. It is very sweet-tasting and doesn't affect the body like sugar. Even diabetics can use stevia. It comes in liquid or powdered form. You don't need to use very much because it is quite strong.

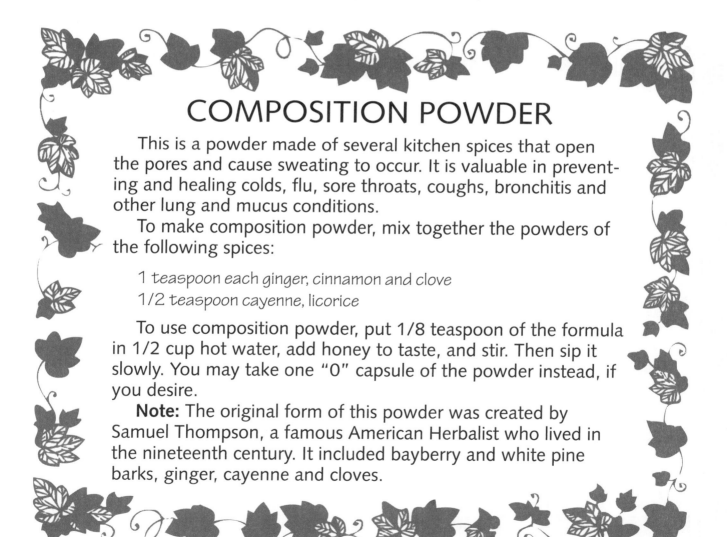

COMPOSITION POWDER

This is a powder made of several kitchen spices that open the pores and cause sweating to occur. It is valuable in preventing and healing colds, flu, sore throats, coughs, bronchitis and other lung and mucus conditions.

To make composition powder, mix together the powders of the following spices:

1 teaspoon each ginger, cinnamon and clove
1/2 teaspoon cayenne, licorice

To use composition powder, put 1/8 teaspoon of the formula in 1/2 cup hot water, add honey to taste, and stir. Then sip it slowly. You may take one "0" capsule of the powder instead, if you desire.

Note: The original form of this powder was created by Samuel Thompson, a famous American Herbalist who lived in the nineteenth century. It included bayberry and white pine barks, ginger, cayenne and cloves.

PLASTERS

A plaster is made by wrapping an herbal mash in a protective cloth, which is then placed on the skin. The cloth or oil is used so the herbs don't burn or irritate the skin. Plasters are described in detail under the herb, garlic. Following are some other plasters you can try.

MUSTARD PLASTER

A mustard pack, or plaster, is a well-known folk remedy used for hundreds of years. It is excellent for aches, sprains, spasms, cold areas needing circulation and to eliminate mucus from the lungs.

Mustard plasters are usually placed on the chest to draw out mucus congestion, dispel coldness, relieve asthma, eliminate coughs and heal colds and flu. They can also be put on other places to treat body and joint aches and pains and heal watery, oozing and chronic sores or boils. To make:

- Mix 1 tablespoon mustard powder, 4 tablespoons whole wheat flour and enough water to form a paste. If the skin is sensitive or if the plaster feels too hot, use an equal amount of egg white instead of the water to prevent blistering.

- Put this paste on a cloth and wrap it up.

- Apply the plaster where desired and leave in place no longer than 10-15 minutes.
  NOTE: Don't leave it on too long or it can burn and cause blistering.

- After removing the plaster, the skin may be powdered with flour and the area wrapped with dry cotton.

ONION PLASTER

Did you know that onions are a natural antibiotic? Because of this, they help heal inflammations and infections. When placed over the lungs, an onion plaster is a tremendous aid to healing pneumonia, lung infections, bronchial inflammation and asthma. It also clears the lungs of mucus congestion and coldness. Placed over the ear for 5 or more minutes, it relieves earaches, too. (The onions can be reheated several times.) To make:

- Slice 1 large onion (preferably organic) and steam until slightly soft.

- Wrap the onion slices in a cloth, then place on the desired area.

- Put a heating pad or hot water bottle on top to keep warm.

- Leave in place 20 minutes.

- Repeat, if desired.

SALT PLASTER

The next time you get an injury from playing baseball, soccer, softball, basketball or any other rough sport, try this simple remedy!

A salt plaster is good for aching or sore muscles and joints. This is because salt holds heat well. It also draws fluid out of the body. Many people find relief from knee pains, tennis elbow or other achy joint pains with this remedy. To make:

- Heat 1/2 cup salt in a dry pan.
- Pour into a bag, or into a dishcloth and tie shut.
- Put directly on the area of pain. Tie in place. Leave on until the salt cools.
- You can repeat this several times if you want.
- If it is too hot, use extra layers of cloth.

MAGICAL TURMERIC BATH

At the first signs of a cold or flu, immediately get into this bath and soak for 20 minutes. Then dry off, dress warmly and get into bed under several covers and rest. It will make you sweat and so is very effective for stopping or breaking colds and flu.

☞ To 1 hot bath add 2-4 tablespoons turmeric powder and 1 teaspoon cayenne powder. Stir well.

☞ Get in and soak! Be sure not to get the bath water in your eyes, or it may sting a bit!

HAVE A COUGH?

Grab that black pepper! Even if you are at a restaurant or a friend's house, you can help your cough go away. Sprinkle a little black pepper powder onto your hand and eat it.

Or mix the black pepper with a little hot water and drink. You can also blend ground black pepper with enough honey to form a paste and eat that, too. It works very quickly.

Try it and see!

TOOTSIE POWDERS

A foot powder is used on the feet to treat fungus or stop itching. It also can help keep the feet warm.

To treat a fungus:

* Combine 1/2 ounce powdered black walnut hulls (a strong antiseptic and anti-fungal), 1/4 ounce powdered calamus root (a deodorizer) and 1/8 ounce sage (an antiseptic and deodorizer).

* Sprinkle this combination on the feet and between the toes before putting on your socks for the day.

To treat itchy feet:

* Powder dried chickweed herb.

* Sprinkle all over the toes before putting your socks on.

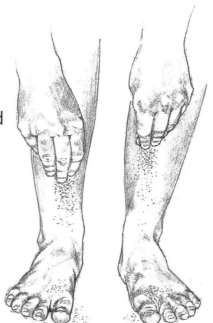

CHINESE FIVE SPICE POWDER

This kitchen powder is very spicy. It is cooked to flavor food such as tofu, poultry and meat. It can also be sprinkled on food as a condiment.

This combination also warms the body up very nicely. It can be taken at the first signs of a cold, flu or cough. Further, it helps clean amoebas and worms out of the intestines. A little Chinese Five Spice powder goes a long way! To use as a medicine:

- Put 1 teaspoon Chinese Five Spice powder into one cup of water.
- Boil covered 5 minutes, then steep 10 minutes.
- Drink, then get under a lot of covers immediately. You will warm up quickly and chase away any colds or flu.

To make Chinese Five Spice Powder, mix together the following:

1/8 cup cinnamon bark powder (the Chinese use cassia bark)

1/8 cup roasted Szechwan peppercorn (This is Zanthozylum pepper. Use regular black peppercorns if the other isn't available.) Roast by putting them in a dry pan. Then heat and stir until toasted.

1/2 cup star anise

1/6 cup fennel seed

1/4 cup cloves

- Grind all spices together in a nut and seed or coffee grinder, blender or food processor.
- Sift the powder through a sieve to get out any unground particles. Regrind them or throw them away.

HERBAL VINEGARS

Vinegars are delicious with oil on salads. They can be made tastier by adding herbs to the vinegar. They look quite beautiful, too, and make nice gifts.

- Put desired herbs into a pretty 12-ounce bottle. You can use a washed-out salad dressing bottle (remove the label).
- Pour white wine vinegar into the bottle until full.
- Cap and store in a cool dark place.

Possible vinegar mixtures:

Spiced vinegar: Use 2-4 garlic cloves, 4-6 ginger slices and 1-2 whole cayenne peppers.

Italian vinegar: Use a whole stem each of rosemary, oregano and thyme and 4-6 leaves of basil.

Dandelion vinegar: Use a handful of dandelion leaves and flowers.

DRINK ONIONS!

Onions are a natural antibiotic. Made into a syrup they are very beneficial for mucus congestion, coughs, bronchitis, colds and flu.

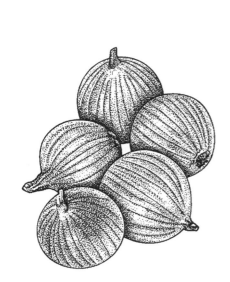

- Simmer 1 medium minced onion in 2 cups water for 20 minutes with enough lemon juice to cover.
- Blend in a food processor or blender.
- Stir in 3 tablespoons honey or brown sugar.
- Add 1/8 teaspoon cayenne pepper.
- Take 1 teaspoonful several times a day, or as needed.
- You may also add a little umeboshi plum paste, too, if desired. This combination soothes tummy aches and treats stomach flu.
- It will keep up to a week when refrigerated.

CAYENNE, KING OF THE KITCHEN SPICES

Cayenne is a wonderful first aid remedy. Because it strongly increases blood circulation, it quickly eases headaches, cramping and diarrhea. It also gives quick energy. Here are some more first aid uses:

🌶 Put directly on bleeding of small cuts. It may sting a little, but it will stop the bleeding.

🌶 Take one "0" capsule with water to help the heart and blood circulation and to ward off colds and flu.

🌶 At the first signs of a cold or flu, put 1-2 teaspoons of cayenne powder in a bathtub full of hot water. Get in and soak. You will begin sweating, but continue soaking for 20 minutes. Immediately dry off, dress in warm clothes and lie down under several blankets. After an hour of sweating, quickly sponge off with cool water, change your clothes and go to bed.

NOTE: Be sure not to get the bath water in your eyes or it may sting!

CLEAR VOICE

Singers often use lemon water to help clear their throats. You can do the same, and heal sore throats or help prevent colds by drinking lemon water with a pinch of cayenne added.

- Squeeze 1 lemon into 2 cups water.
- Stir in 1/16-1/8 teaspoon of cayenne powder.
- Sweeten with honey.
- Drink throughout the day.
- If this tastes too spicy, then take one "0" capsule of cayenne with the lemon-honey-water.

HOT TOOTSIES

To keep your feet warm, put on a thin pair of socks. Then sprinkle some cayenne powder into a second pair of thick socks. Pull the second pair on over the first.

If you do this before going outside to play on a cold day, your feet will stay toasty warm! (Be sure to wash your hands immediately after putting on the second pair of socks.)

TIGER SAUCE

Here is a spicy blend that is also a delicious sauce on your food!

It can also be taken by itself to warm you up. Just put 5-10 drops in water and drink. Soon your body will be tingling all over. Tiger sauce can be taken at the first signs of a sore throat, cold or flu to prevent them from developing.

Rub the tiger sauce onto any bruises, sore muscles or aching joints you may have. Be sure to rinse your hands immediately afterwards or else it might get into your eyes. (This won't hurt your eyes, but it will make them sting for a while. Then when the stinging stops, your eyes will be clear and bright!)

Mix together well:
- 1/2 cup apple cider vinegar
- 1 tablespoon garlic powder
- 1 teaspoon cayenne pepper
- 1/4 teaspoon salt

PEPPER CHAIN

Cayenne peppers are such a vibrant red color that they make a beautiful decoration, which is useful as well.

- Thread a needle with a long, thick, double thread.
- Thread each pepper on the string by sewing through the top of the pepper.
- Tie a knot at the end and hang the pepper chain in the kitchen. Whenever a pepper is needed in cooking, simply cut one off the string and retie the knot.

NOTE: It is best to wear gloves when handling cayenne. If you get it on your hands, do not touch your face, eyes, nose or mouth, for it will sting. Rinse with cool water should you get it on your hands or face.

SING ALONG!

Cayenne Song
Michael Tierra

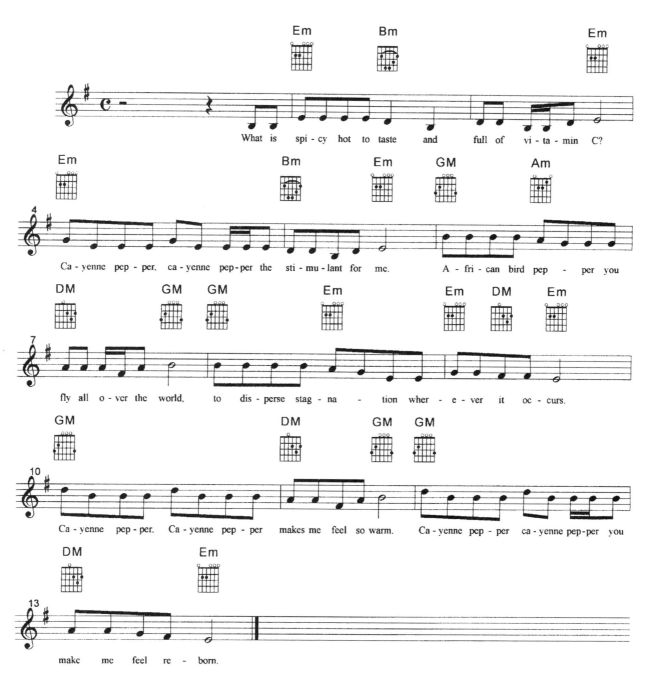

STORY TIME!
Cay and the Fire

There once lived a young warrior named Cay. Strong and skillful, he was also very handsome. Yet he bragged all the time, and thought he was the best at everything. At first the other children put up with this because they admired Cay's strength and skill. But his constant bragging and winning all their games made them feel unhappy. Eventually, Cay didn't have any friends at all.

One day, when the villagers were tired of his behavior, they created an impossible challenge so as to be rid of him: Cay had to get an eye tooth from a tiger, and he could not return to the village until he had done so. Confident and happy, Cay accepted the ordeal, for he thought it would make him a hero.

Cay searched wide and far. An expert hunter, he found plenty of game, but oddly, never once did he see a tiger. After several years Cay became lonely and discouraged with his failure. This forced him to think about his life. He realized he was self-centered, unkind, and never thought of anyone but himself. For the first time in his life, Cay knew he needed help.

Cay cried out long and hard to the Great Spirit, "Please! Help me to change my ways! Help me learn to live in harmony with all people!" Suddenly, a medicine man appeared and said he had been magically sent to help Cay. He said there was a special ceremony they could perform that would help Cay change. Cay gratefully accepted.

When it was dark, Cay and the medicine man built a very large fire. Then the medicine man told Cay to think about all the old behaviors he wanted to change. Cay thought about boasting, acting like he was better than everyone else and always having to win when he played games. He thought of the people he hadn't respected and all the friends he had lost. Finally, he thought of how lonely and selfish he had become as a result.

When the medicine man saw Cay was ready, he said, "Now give these thoughts, feelings and old behavior to the fire, Cay. Ask the fire to help you change."

Cay had to use all his inner strength and skill to focus on this task. As he imagined all his old feelings and behaviors flying out of him into the fire, the flames leapt higher and higher into the night sky. Soon, the fire was roaring furiously, and its increasing heat threatened to burn Cay.

Then, abruptly, the fire flung large drops of flames into the bright night. They fell like a hot shower of rain to the earth. This went on all night. It was nearly dawn before Cay became weary, and the fire died down.

Exhausted, Cay fell to the ground. Although tired, he felt that all his old feelings were gone. In their place a soothing peace surged through his body. Cay was filled with thanks for the wonder of all life. As the sun rose, Cay looked around and was startled to see a new plant growing everywhere in sight. It had a strange red fruit.

The medicine man said, "The fire has changed your old behavior into a gift for people. This new plant has a fruit which carries your strength and zeal. Yet it heals rather than hurts. Go, take it back to your village to share with your tribe."

Cay returned to his tribe with the red fruit. It was shaped exactly like a tiger's eye tooth. It had a sharp and biting taste, also like the tiger. The fruit healed many illnesses and helped his people. When the villagers saw how this gift represented the miraculous change in Cay, they named the pepper Cayenne, after him. In time Cay grew wise and generous, and his life became filled with happiness and friends.

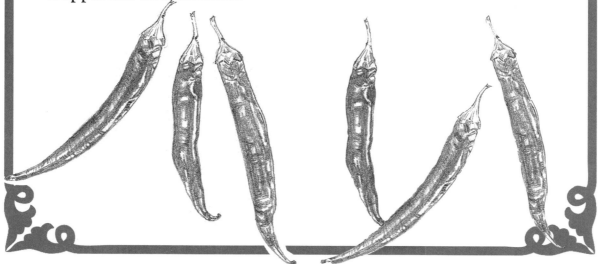

5

FLOWER POWER

Don't you just love flowers? They are not only beautiful to look at, but smell wonderful, too. Flowers show our love for others when we give them as gifts on birthdays or other special times. Yet flowers also have many other wonderful uses. Here are a few of them.

EATING FLOWERS?

Have you ever sucked the nectar out of the end of a honeysuckle flower? It is sweet and delicious. Many flowers can actually be eaten. Most flowers are mild in flavor, but some can be a bit spicy, like nasturtiums.

Try mixing flowers in your salad. This makes a colorful and unique salad blend and creates interesting flavors. Or put a few brilliant purple-blue borage flowers on top of your favorite dessert or on waffles or pancakes. Lemon blossoms added to lemonade make it taste even more lemony.

Flowers you can eat: violets, nasturtiums, honeysuckle, borage, pansies, rose or calendula petals, elder, mustard, chive and onion blossoms, Johnny-jump-ups, clover, apple blossoms, mullein, chrysanthemum, mallow, squash blossoms, pinks, forget-me-nots, fennel, rosemary, thyme, dill, lavender flowers, day lilies.

Caution: Remember that not all flowers are safe to eat. Oleanders are quite poisonous. Never eat a flower unless it has been identified as being safe by an adult first.

DID YOU KNOW . . .

Flowers have healing power, too. Many flowers have valuable properties and are given as medicine, usually as a tea. We talked about flowers that are used as herbs: chamomile, mullein and calendula. Here are some more flowers and their healing uses:

Honeysuckle: fevers, colds, flu, skin problems, infections, inflammations, viruses, sore throats, hot painful eyes, swellings, headaches

Chrysanthemum: headaches across the forehead, red eyes, fevers

Magnolia: the buds are used to open the nose during colds, sinus infections or allergies

Safflower: measles, rashes; it stimulates blood circulation, stops bleeding from wounds

Passion flower: insomnia, nervousness, tension

Carnation (pinks): bladder infections, constipation

Red clover: skin eruptions, eczema, fevers and blood purification

CANDIED FLOWERS

Not too long ago people frequently ate candied violets and rose petals. They are really delicious. Although they can still be purchased from some specialty shops, they are fairly easy to make. Here's how:

- ❀ First, pick the flowers you want to candy. Very, very gently rinse them with water, then set them to dry on a towel.

- ❀ Make a syrup by boiling 2/3 cup granulated sugar (unrefined cane sugar is best) and 1/2 cup water.

- ❀ Boil the mixture about 5-10 minutes, stirring occasionally, until it forms a light syrup.

- ❀ Using a fork or tongs, dip each flower into the syrup. Gently shake off the excess. Set flowers on a cookie sheet covered with waxed paper.

- ❀ With a toothpick, straighten out any folded or bent petals.

- ❀ Let flowers dry in a warm place out of the sun.

- ❀ Store them carefully in a tin until ready to eat.

Good flowers to candy: violets, rose petals, borage, honeysuckle.

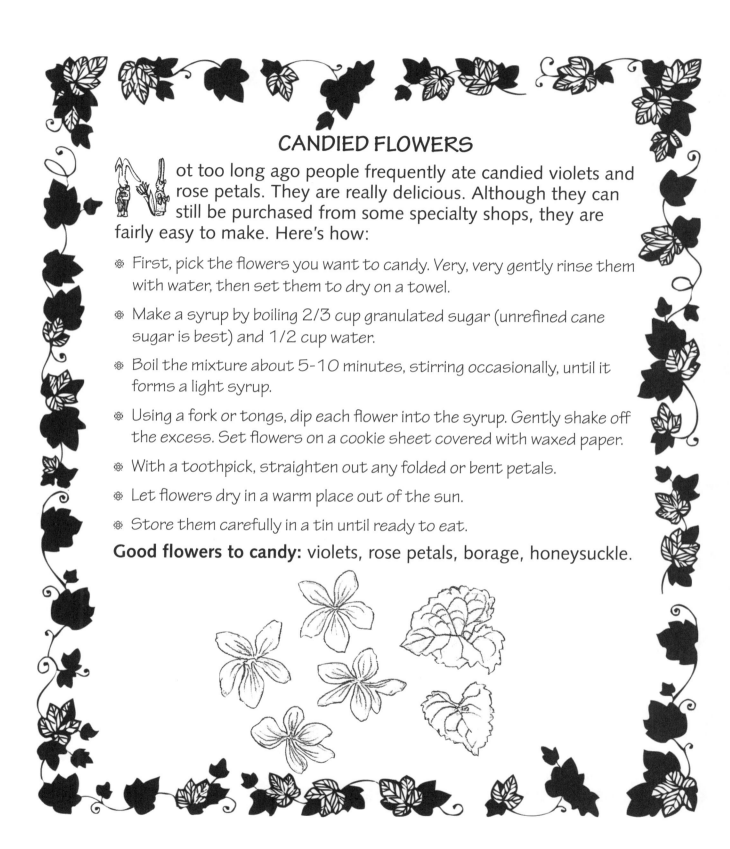

FLOWER VINEGAR

Vinegars have long been combined with herbs to create a special taste for salads. A simple flower vinegar can be made by stuffing a bottle or jar with a mixture of edible flowers, such as rosemary flowers, nasturtiums, violets, borage or thyme flowers, and then pouring white wine vinegar into the jar until it is full. Shake it up every day. It will be ready for use in two weeks.

FLOWER POWER TEA

Make a tea of your favorite flowers! Choose flowers according to their uses as medicine, or according to their color and shape. To make the tea:

- Stuff a small teapot full of your chosen flowers (or use 1 table-spoon dried flowers).

- Bring 1 cup water to a boil.

- Pour the boiling water over the flowers in the teapot. Cover with a lid.

- Let sit for 10-20 minutes.

- Strain. Add honey to taste. Enjoy!

FLOWER MEDICINE

Flowers that have a strong odor have a lot of volatile oils. These oils hold the scent of the flower. Called essential oils, they are used in perfumes, added to candles and soaps to make them smell good and used as a healing therapy called aromatherapy.

DRYING FLOWERS

ried flowers keep a very long time so you can enjoy them over and over again. They can be used to make beautiful dried flower bouquets. The best flowers to dry are large and thick. Small flowers keep better pressed.

There are two methods:

1) Pick your flowers early in the day. Then carefully tie them together with a string at the bottom of their stems. In a dark, airy place, tack the other end of the string to the ceiling, top of a wall or tie to a beam. Hang until dry, usually about two weeks.

2) For more brightly colored dry flowers, dry them in sand. Sand is one of the oldest methods for drying flowers.

- First, layer the bottom of a shoe box or cookie tin with sand. Then set the flowers on top, blossoms facing up.

- Gently sprinkle sand over them until they are covered. Use a toothpick if necessary to get the sand into all the crevices so the flowers dry well.

- Seal the box by taping the lid on.

- Set in a warm dry place. Flowers keep their color well and may be kept in the sand a long time without causing any damage. But wait at least two to four weeks before removing.

If sand isn't available, you can also use two parts cornmeal to one part borax (available in grocery stores), or clean, unscented kitty litter.

PRESSING FLOWERS

Smaller flowers are best dried when pressed flat. Then they can be used to decorate many different things: bookmarks, note cards, diaries, writing paper, calendars, scrapbooks. They can even be made into pictures.

- Choose flowers that are fresh and moisture-free.

- Cut the flowers you want from their stems near the base of the flower. Wait until later in the day to do this, when the dew has dried.

- Lay down a piece of cardboard on the table. Place a sheet of blotting paper on the cardboard. (Purchase blotting paper from art, drug or office supply stores.)

- Space flowers on the blotting paper so they don't touch each other. With your fingertips press down on the flowers gently to help spread out their petals.

- Cover with another sheet of blotting paper then put a piece of cardboard on top.

- Continue layering cardboard and blotting paper while spreading the flowers apart on the blotting paper. End with cardboard on top of the entire stack.

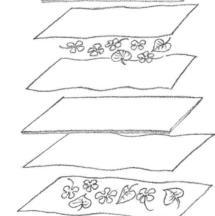

- Place the stack out of the way on a counter, floor or table. Then set several heavy books on top of the stack.

- Leave the pile alone for two weeks. You may want to check the flowers after the first day to see if the petals need rearranging.

- After two weeks, remove the books from the stack.

- Gently pull the layers apart. To use the flowers, carefully pull each off the blotting paper.

Note: Commercial flower presses are available and come in several sizes. They are often sold in stores or through catalogs.

QUICK PRESS

A quick flower press can be made by using an old telephone book. Simply lay the flowers carefully down between several of the pages, close the book and set several other heavy books on top. Leave for 2-3 weeks, when they should be dry.

FLOWER STATIONERY, NOTECARDS, CALENDARS OR SCRAPBOOKS

Wouldn't it be special to write letters on paper that is decorated with delicately pressed flowers? Or have dried flowers arranged on your scrapbook or adorning your calendar?

You can do all of this easily with a few pressed flowers and some clear-drying glue. Here's how:

- Press and dry the flowers you want. You can also dry leaves, ivy, ferns or clover.

- Using a clear-drying glue, glue flowers onto note card paper, stationery, a calendar or scrapbook in a pleasing arrangement.

- Decorate the entire front, or the top, bottom, or border as desired.

FRAME IT!

Make a framed flower picture by decorating the background card or paper of a ready-made picture frame with a variety of pressed flowers. Arrange in an interesting design. Choose contrasting colors and a mix of different flowers.

Then insert the decorated paper back into the frame. Now you have a beautiful picture of your favorite flowers.

FLOWER BOOKMARK

Creating your own flowered bookmark is not only easy, it also makes reading even more fun than it already is!

- Cut a rectangular piece of colored construction paper any size you wish.

- Write your name, the date and the name of the flowers used on one side.

- Glue the dried flowers in a pretty design. You can add dried ferns, leaves and grasses, too, if you'd like.

- Cover with clear contact paper or lamination paper.

- Punch a hole in the top, and tie a ribbon through it.

POTPOURRI (PO-POUR-E)

A potpourri is a mixture of dried herbs that is sweet-smelling and pretty to see. Usually the dried herbs are loosely mixed together in a bowl or glass jar. They are then set on a table as a decoration and to scent the room.

❖ Dry the flowers you want to use. Be sure to cut off the stems first.

❖ Gently mix together the dried flowers in a non-metallic bowl.

❖ Add 1 teaspoon powdered or chopped orris root to 1 cup dried herbal mixture. Orris root fixes the herbs so they look and smell good a long time. Orris root can be purchased at an herbal store. If you can't find orris root, use powdered calamus root.

❖ If desired, add a few drops of scented oil to make the mixture smell even better.

❖ Pour the herbs into a bowl, glass container or small basket. Place a lid on the container to keep the scent longer.

❖ Set the container in a room to give it a lovely look and fresh smell. Take the lid off when you wish to smell the herbs and scent the room.

❖ If the scent begins to fade after a while, stir the mixture or add another drop or two of scented oil.

POTPOURRI AND SACHET FLOWERS AND SCENTS

There are a number of herbs that can be used for potpourris and sachets. Use a variety and blend them together with an eye to interesting combinations of color, shape and size.

Flowers: calendula, yarrow, lemon balm, chamomile, rose buds and petals, borage, lavender, rosemary, jasmine, honeysuckle, orange blossoms, lilac, statice, red clover, carnation, miniature chrysanthemums.

Barks and Peels: orange peel, cinnamon bark, cloves, allspice.

Spices: nutmeg, cloves, allspice, cardamom.

Other Herbs: bay leaves, vanilla beans.

Scented oils: choose any flower or herb oils you like.

FRAGRANT SACHETS (SAH-SHAY)

Sachets are mixtures of sweet-smelling dried herbs that are wrapped in pretty cloth or lace. Then they are placed in dresser drawers or hung in closets to make the clothes smell good.

* Follow the first four steps for making potpourris.

* Pour the herbs into muslin bags, or make your own bags from colored fabric or lace. Tie closed with a ribbon to form a pouch.

* Place in dresser drawers or hang in closets or on doorknobs.

213

HATS OFF!

Take your favorite hat off—it's time to decorate it!

Garlands have adorned people's heads for centuries. After Olympic races in Greece, victors were given laurel garlands to wear. Garlands were also given to Roman actors following an outstanding performance. That is why flowers are still presented today to musicians or actors after they perform. People also wore garlands to celebrate the beginning of spring.

Here are three ways to make a garland. Choose the one you like best. A flowered hat is made by attaching the garland to the crown of the hat.

1) Braid together three branches of willow, bay or fern. Make the braid long enough to encircle the top of a hat. Tie both ends together with a piece of ribbon, leaving the ends long for streamers, or tie them into a bow. Add flowers by weaving their stems into the braid.

2) Using florists' wire, make a thin wire circle to snugly fit the top of the hat. Bunch together 3 or 4 flowers and wrap with a ribbon onto the wire band. Continue around the circle, overlapping the flowers. Slip the finished band over the hat. Tie 2 pieces of ribbon at the back of the hat as streamers.

3) Using florists' wire, make a thin wire circle to snugly fit the top of the hat. Attach silk flowers to the wire ring with florists' tape. Encircle the hat with 1/2-1 inch wide ribbon. Stitch the ribbon to the hat in several places around the crown to hold it in place. Put the ring of flowers over the ribbon and stitch it to the hat to secure it. Add ribbons for streamers.

Flowers and herbs to use: yarrow, statice, bay, rosemary, lavender, strawflowers.

214

6
LET'S HAVE A TEA PARTY!

Tea parties are so much fun. People in many countries, such as the United Kingdom, go to a tea shop in the late afternoons. There they might have a "simple" tea of scones, butter, whipped cream and jam. Or they might have a "high" tea of tiny tea sandwiches, meat, vegetables, cheese, breads and luscious desserts such as tortes, cakes, pies and cookies.

You can create a tea shop right in your own home by having a tea party. Invite several friends over to share in the occasion. You can have it at tea time—about 4 p.m.—or any time of day you choose.

Getting ready for the party can be as much fun as the party itself! Perhaps you will want to dress up and ask your friends to dress up, too. Set up small tea tables (use card tables) in your living room or out on a patio, in the backyard or garden area if the weather is nice.

Then serve your favorite foods, all cooked and decorated with herbs. To help you do this, several special herbal recipes are included here. You can follow these recipes, or create your own. Be creative! Imagine different foods with herbs and try them. And just think, as you are eating these special foods, the herbs are bringing you and your friends good health!

FLOWERED INVITATIONS

Send out invitations to your tea party. Use note cards decorated with pressed flowers. Be sure to include the date, time and place of your party.

You might even sprinkle some lavender blossoms or rose petals into the envelope with your invitation. Then when your friends open their cards they'll enjoy a lovely flower fragrance as well.

DECORATE YOUR PARTY

Decorate the tea tables and eating area. Use fresh flowers, ivy, ferns, houseplants and other plants. Perhaps set a rose at each place. Hang plantain window pictures in the windows. Set out bowls of sweet-smelling potpourris. Have a yarrow dried flower bouquet and a basket garden nearby. These are just suggestions—you can come up with your own decorative ideas, too.

PLACE CARDS

At very formal dinner parties each person's name is written on a card and set at a given place on the table. Then people sit where their place card is set.

You can do the same at your tea party:

* Fold a small card in half, so it will stand up by itself.
* Write each friend's name on one half of the card.
* Decorate the card with pressed flowers.
* Set them on the tables at the head of the silverware settings. Then your friends will know where to sit.

MENU CARDS

Let your friends know what they are eating by having a menu card for each table. List all the food and drinks you are serving. Then decorate the menu cards with pressed flowers in a decorative design. Set on each table at the beginning of the tea party.

HERBAL RECIPES

Herbs are wonderful cooked in food. They give flavor, color and beauty and can even help prevent or heal a cold or flu!

Here are several herbal foods and drinks you can serve at your tea party. Choose to make one, several, or all of the recipes as you desire. Create some of your own recipes and serve those, too.

Decorate the food as well. Arrange fresh flowers on the platters or on top of the food. Put a candied flower on each plate.

CUCUMBER AND WATERCRESS SANDWICHES

Watercress grows beside rivers, streams or brooks in cool places. It is often put in salads or soups. Its cooling energy is refreshing on a hot summer day.

* Trim the crust off several pieces of thinly sliced bread. Spread a thin layer of cream cheese on all of them.

* Top some of the bread pieces with paper-thin slices of cucumber and others with sprigs of watercress.

* Cover with another piece of bread spread with cream cheese.

* Cut the sandwiches into triangles or squares.

* Decorate the top of each tiny sandwich with a sprig of parsley or a watercress leaf.

Basil Pesto

This can be prepared ahead of time and refrigerated. It keeps for several weeks. You can also freeze it. Spread it on bread or crackers. (Of course it can also be mixed with spaghetti noodles for dinner some night!)

3 packed cups fresh basil leaves
3 cloves garlic
1/4 cup pine nuts or walnuts
3/4 cup parmesan cheese, grated
1/2-3/4 cup olive oil
1/2 packed cup parsley

❖ Puree everything together in a blender or food processor.

❖ Pour into a container and cover with 2 tablespoons oil to keep it from darkening.

Flowered Salad

Colored flowers are striking against green leaves in a flower salad. They also add a gentle fragrance and slightly spicy-sweet taste to the salad.

❖ Wash and dry edible flowers such as chives, nasturtiums, violets, borage, pansies, wild radish, Johnny-jump-ups, rose and calendula petals. Add to salad greens.

❖ Sprinkle with your favorite dressing and toss all together.

Violet Honey

Although this recipe needs to be made ahead of time, it keeps a long time. It also makes a great gift.

❖ Fill a jar half full of violets (other edible flowers may also be used, such as roses, pinks or honeysuckle.)

❖ Fill the jar with honey.

❖ Leave at least 10 days in a warm place.

❖ Eat the violets with the honey.

Herbed Scones

Add 1 tablespoon rosemary flowers and leaves, dill, thyme, basil, sweet marjoram or other herbal flowers and leaves to a scone or biscuit recipe.

. . . .

Rose Petal Jam

2½ cups water
1½ cups fresh or ¾ cup dried rose petals
1-2 teaspoons rose water (Optional: Purchase in grocery stores where flavored extracts are kept.)
1 small lemon, juiced
2-4 tablespoons honey to taste
1½ tablespoons cornstarch

❖ Blend together 1½ cups water, rose petals, rose water (if used), lemon juice and honey.

❖ Dissolve cornstarch in 1 cup water. Add to rose mixture. A layer of rose petals and frothy liquid may separate on top of the jam; remove this before jam sets.

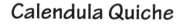

❖ Pour into jars and refrigerate for immediate use.

. . . .

Calendula Quiche

1 pie crust
1/4-1/3 lb. cheese (Monterey Jack, Cheddar and Swiss cheese are good choices.)
1 cup chopped onions
calendula petals from 8-10 calendulas
3 eggs
1 cup milk

* Grate cheese and put in pie crust.

* Sauté onions and mix with calendula petals. Pour over cheese.

* Beat together eggs and milk. Pour over top of pie mixture.

* Bake 35-40 minutes at 375 degrees F.

* Let cool. Cut into 6-8 pie wedges. Top each with a calendula flower.

Candied Flowers

Follow the recipe under candied flowers in Chapter 5, "Flower Power." Try violets, honeysuckle, rose petals and borage flowers.

Ginger Cookies

Follow the ginger cookie recipe given with the herb ginger in Chapter 2, "The Secret Gifts of Herbs."

Ginger-ale Fizz

Follow the ginger-ale fizz recipe given with the herb ginger in Chapter 2, "The Secret Gifts of Herbs."

Lemon Balm Sun Tea

Follow the recipe given with the herb lemon balm in Chapter 2, "The Secret Gifts of Herbs."

Fennel Candy

Follow the recipe given with the herb fennel in Chapter 2, "The Secret Gifts of Herbs."

PARTY GIFTS

It's always a special treat to receive a gift when you go to a party, isn't it? Make herbal gifts to give away at the end of your tea party. There are all sorts of herbal gifts to give away—sachets, dried flower bouquets, a jar of herbal salve, dream pillows, yarrow pick-up-sticks, flowered stationery, fennel toothpowder ... these are just a few of many possibilities.

You could also play some games at your tea party, and use any of these gift ideas as prizes. Then at the very end of the party, give a sachet or other herbal gift to each friend.

7

Gardens Galore!

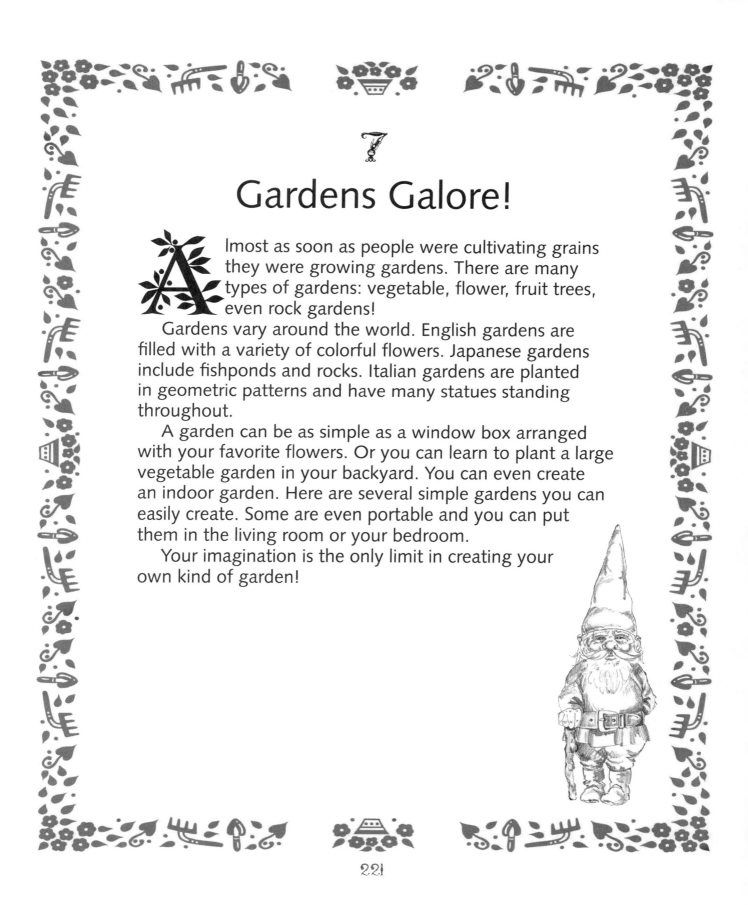

Almost as soon as people were cultivating grains they were growing gardens. There are many types of gardens: vegetable, flower, fruit trees, even rock gardens!

Gardens vary around the world. English gardens are filled with a variety of colorful flowers. Japanese gardens include fishponds and rocks. Italian gardens are planted in geometric patterns and have many statues standing throughout.

A garden can be as simple as a window box arranged with your favorite flowers. Or you can learn to plant a large vegetable garden in your backyard. You can even create an indoor garden. Here are several simple gardens you can easily create. Some are even portable and you can put them in the living room or your bedroom.

Your imagination is the only limit in creating your own kind of garden!

WINDOW BOX GARDEN

This is similar to a Potted Bouquet, but instead of a flowerpot, use a long narrow flower box or plastic-lined basket about 6" wide by 18" to 24" long. You may have one at home, or you can purchase one from a nursery or garden center. It can be planted with flowers or herbs. This makes a good kitchen garden, too, when planted with culinary herbs. Set outside or inside the window to decorate the kitchen or dining area. To make a window box garden, follow the directions for a Potted Bouquet (pg. 224).

BULB GARDEN

Bulb gardens make colorful indoor gardens because they flower in the winter and spring. Fall and early winter are the best time to plant bulb gardens. Follow the directions for a Potted Bouquet, but use bulbs instead.

- Plant 2 bulbs in an 8" sized flowerpot and 3 bulbs in a 12" sized flowerpot. Set the bulbs deep into the soil with the pointed, growing end on top.
- Cover with 1"-2" soil.
- Water weekly.

Possible bulbs: amaryllis, narcissus, daffodils, hyacinth, begonias, freesia, tulips.

FIRST AID GARDEN

There is a type of cactus, aloe vera, whose leaves contain a gooey fluid that is very healing. If anyone gets burned, immediately cut off a piece of the aloe leaf (be careful of its rough edges) and squeeze some of its clear fluid onto the burn. Within minutes the pain will go away.

Aloe heals the skin. It is excellent for skin irritations or outbreaks, some types of eczema and cuts. It has been used all over the world as a face cream, shampoo and burn ointment.

- Purchase an aloe vera plant from a nursery.
- Set on a kitchen counter or table. It grows very well indoors.

SPICE GARDEN

row a garden full of herbs you can use in cooking! Herbs used in this way are called culinary herbs. They flavor food so it tastes good. Many culinary herbs also help the digestion.

A kitchen garden grown outdoors in the ground can include fennel, rosemary, garlic and cayenne. Many kitchen herbs can be grown indoors as a window box garden. Use basil, thyme, sage, oregano, chives, parsley, coriander or cilantro.

To use fresh herbs in cooking, just pinch off the amount you need and strip the leaves from the stems. These herbs can also be dried and stored for future use or gifts.

To dry the herbs, place the stripped leaves on a screen in a warm dry place out of the sun (try your attic!) Turn them over once or twice a week. Within a few weeks they should be dry. Store in clean glass bottles out of the sun and away from heat. Be sure to label and date your jars.

Flowers that grow well in window boxes: gardenias, nasturtiums, petunias, impatiens, carnations. Almost any short herb or flower does well in a window box.

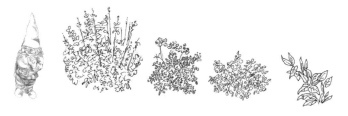

BASKET GARDEN

This creates a beautiful inside garden. It is easy to do and you can change it throughout the year to match the seasons. It also makes a lovely gift.

1 large basket
1 or more plastic dishes that fit inside the basket
Plants
Spanish moss (get at a florist or nursery)

✧ Line the basket with the dishes. This makes the basket waterproof.
✧ Set the plants in the basket with 1 plant in the center and several around the edge.
✧ Water plants carefully.
✧ Tuck Spanish moss around the basket, the pot edges and in between the pots.
✧ Set on a table, such as a dining or coffee table, or on a desktop, dresser or kitchen counter.

Plants to use: Ivy, ferns, household plants, potted flowers.

POTTED BOUQUET

Make a colorful living bouquet in a pot! It lasts longer than cut flowers and can be put indoors or outdoors depending on the flowers used. To make one you will need several items from a nursery or garden store.

    12" or larger flowerpot
    Small rocks or pebbles to fill the flowerpot 1" deep
    Potting soil
    Trowel
    Plants

- Put the pebbles in the bottom of the pot. They help hold the soil in and allow drainage for the plant's roots.
- Fill the pot with potting soil. Stop about 2" from the rim.
- Plan a pretty arrangement, allowing for your plants to be set into the pot a few inches apart from each other. Remove the plants from their nursery pots. Push the soil aside to make space for each plant. Set the plant in the hole, then gently press the soil around it to hold it in place.
- Place the flowerpot in a dish and set in a sunny spot.
- Water well, then water the plants every other day, or whenever the soil feels dry.
- Pick off the flowers when they wither. This encourages the plant to grow more flowers.

Flowers to use: You can plant any flower or herb in a pot, but not trees or other plants that grow very tall. Some common flowers that make a pretty bouquet include geranium, pansy, alyssum, chrysanthemum, African violets, cyclamen, daisies, baby's breath.

Annuals: These are plants that bloom all summer and then die.

Perennials: These are plants which bloom for a while and then reappear, year after year.

COMPOST

Compost is made from dead plant material made from kitchen scraps, yard clippings, fertilizer and soil. Over time, this mixture decays to create compost. It is like food for the soil because it is loaded with vitamins and minerals. Some people call it 'black gold' because this is what makes rich and fertile soil in which the plants can grow healthy and strong.

1. Using an old garbage can for your compost, punch several small holes in the bottom and the sides first. (It is important that air mixes with the materials to create compost.) Set near your garden area.

2. Make compost with:

- Kitchen scraps: vegetable clippings, coffee grounds, egg shells, fruit rinds, etc.
- Yard scraps: garden plant clippings, grass clippings, leaves
- Fertilizer: horse, cow or chicken manure
- Lime (get from a nursery)

3. To create a layer, mix kitchen scraps with yard scraps; sprinkle with manure and lime. Cover this layer with a thinner one of soil. Start a new layer, just like the first, creating it over time as kitchen and yard scraps become available. Water this mixture frequently to speed decay. Allow the mixture to compost for 3-6 months before using.

4. Stir the compost periodically to give it air. Keep it moist, but not wet. Cover the can with a lid or layer of soil or peat moss. This keeps flies away. If you do these three things, your compost should smell sweet and earthy and not rotten.

MULCH

Mulch is placed around plants to help keep the soil moist. Then it doesn't dry out too quickly from the hot sun. Mulch also slows the growth of weeds around your plants.

Good materials for mulch include:

- partially decomposed compost
- leaves
- straw
- barley or rice hulls

A PLOT OF YOUR OWN

Create your own herb garden! You can use a space in your backyard or create a small plot in one of the flower beds. Plant it with a variety of herbs. Some of them you can grow from seeds, like fennel or cayenne. Others, such as dandelion, yarrow or plantain, you can transplant from yards, ditches or vacant lots. Often a neighbor friend may have some herbs growing and you can get cuttings from them to grow in your own garden.

* Dig up the soil in your garden area. It needs to be loose so the plants can grow well.

* Add in some manure or compost and mix it well with the soil. This provides food for the plants. Manure can be purchased at nurseries, or you can make your own compost.

* Plant your seeds by following the directions on the package. To plant herb cuttings, transplants or herbs in pots, first make deep and wide depressions in the soil. Then set the plants into the depressions. Hold the plants by their leaves, not their stems. If the stem breaks, it's goodbye plant! Fill in the holes with the surrounding soil and pat down to remove any air holes.

* Place mulch over the ground around the plants. Do not cover the leaves or stems of the plants. Mulch helps the soil retain moisture longer.

* Be sure to water your plants regularly. In fact, watering the garden before and after you plant helps the plants grow stronger.

* End with good wishes that your plants grow well!

DESIGN YOUR OWN GARDEN

Try designing your garden first on paper before planting it. Use different colors for each plant you want. Leave space between the plants.

Gardens are usually planted in rows, but try different shapes such as a circle or diamond. Then you can outline your garden shape with large rocks or shells, if you wish.

CREATING YOUR OWN HERB GARDEN

Consider these possibilities in planting your garden:

* Try planting seeds purchased from a nursery.

* Plant seedling starts, also purchased from a nursery.

* Use cuttings from existing plants— get them from neighbors or friends.

* Replant herbs from pots into the garden.

* Add ornamental flowers for beauty.

* Arrange plants according to their colors and height.

* Include herbs used in cooking such as thyme, oregano, rosemary, basil and coriander.

* Include herbs you don't know yet in order to learn about them.

LEARNING FROM YOUR GARDEN

If you watch your plants grow each day you can learn a lot about them. Here are ideas of things to watch for:

- What color are each plant's leaves? flowers?

- When does each plant like to flower?

- Do the flowers stay open all day and night? Or do they close at night? or close during the day?

- In what shape and pattern do the leaves grow?

- How many petals do the flowers have? In what pattern are they arranged?

- Do some plants like more water than others?

- Do some plants grow easily while others need more care?

- Which plants like a lot of sun? shade?

8

Herbs Need Our Help, Too

Herbs grow all over the place—in back yards, between sidewalk cracks, in store window boxes, as house plants. Even in cities you can find plants growing if you only look for them.

While plants grow all by themselves, they thrive when humans help them along. They love to be watered, given sunlight or shade, to be fed and weeded so they have more room to grow.

Plants also need to be protected—from chemical spills, garbage, needless digging and water and air pollution. You can learn to help the plants, trees and flowers in your area by giving them what they need and by removing what is harmful to them.

THE CYCLE OF LIFE

Many things feed the earth—sunshine, rain, the moon and stars, decaying plant material, animal manure—on and on the list grows. As the earth is fed, it is enriched and better able to grow seeds. Plants, herbs, flowers, trees, all grow out of this fertile soil.

Plants provide shelter, clothing, food, medicines and much more, for all humans and animals. In turn, human garbage and animal manure can nourish the earth when prepared as compost. Compost feeds the earth along with sun and rain, continuing the cycle. (To make compost, see Chapter 7)

Ecosystems

Ecosystems are particular places on earth in which certain living things have come to live together. The study of ecosystems is called ecology. Ecologists study the relationships between living things and their environments.

An ecosystem has living and non-living things. A desert ecosystem contains non-living things such as sand, dirt, rocks and sunlight. It also has living things such as snakes, scorpions, greasewood (chaparral) and sagebrush.

A coastal ocean ecosystem has sand, rocks, salt water, ocean currents and shipwrecks along with starfish, seaweed, water plants, fish and dolphins.

An urban ecosystem, such as you might have in your back yard, probably contains soil, dirt, rocks, ants, snails, lizards, and lots of different weeds like dandelions and plantain.

Gaia – cycle of life

compost

plants

THE FOOD CHAIN

Sunlight is the energy source that powers all ecosystems' food chains. A food chain shows how energy is passed from one living thing to another. It is also made up of living things which eat one another to stay alive.

All things are connected! If one link in the chain is taken out, the whole food chain is affected. Over and over a farmer puts poison on the weeds to kill them. In time the birds are gone. Why? Because the food chain was broken.

The birds didn't eat the weeds, but the weeds were home to the worms and snails which birds did eat. When the weeds were killed, so were the worms and snails which the birds ate. Either the birds died from lack of food or left to find food elsewhere. If we disturb an ecosystem, we destroy its food chain.

THINGS PEOPLE DO THAT HARM ECOSYSTEMS:

1. Use poisonous chemicals on weeds to kill them.

2. Over-harvest plants.

3. Remove native plants.

4. Introduce plants from foreign areas, which then take over and force out the native plants.

5. Dump chemicals, sewage and garbage on the area.

232

What can I do to help plants and their ecosystems?

Plants and their ecosystems need our help! When humans disturb an ecosystem, plant life there dies. There are many things to do to help your local ecosystem. The following are just a few ideas. Come up with your own plans as well to suit your local environmental needs.

ADOPT AN ECOSYSTEM!

our backyard is an ecosystem. So is a vacant lot near you, or farm land or a park area. Adopting an ecosystem means you are going to care for the land and its plants over time. If you cannot continue to care for it, you won't abandon the area. You will find other people to care for it in your place.

Pick an area of plants near you. Choose one area that is not too big so you can properly care for it. The area could be a flowerbed, your yard, a strip of land near you, a vacant lot (ask the owner for permission). If you live in a city, choose a local park or beach.

OBSERVE THESE HABITS IN YOUR ADOPTED ECOSYSTEM:

Leave habitat in place:

If you turn over a stone to observe spiders or bugs living underneath, gently roll the stone back in place.

Encourage native plants:

Native plants are the plants that are supposed to live in an ecosystem. They are especially suited to the weather and soil. Leave native plants where they are. Plant more native plants in the area. Do not plant non-native plants that are invasive.

Don't over-harvest:

When harvesting plants, just take a few from each stand. Always leave several plants in an area so they can perpetuate themselves.

Keep garbage and poisons out of the ecosystem:

Pull weeds instead of spraying them. If you see garbage in the area, clean it up. Oil, gasoline, bleach, paint, cleaning solutions, pesticides and herbicides are poisons. If you see evidence of any poisons in your ecosystem, immediately report it to an adult and ask for the area to be cleaned.

DO NOT HANDLE POISONS or anything
you suspect to be a poison.
Always notify an adult and ask for help.

GARDEN YOUR ECOSYSTEM

Beautify your local ecosystem. Plant trees, flowers, vegetables and herbs. Be creative! Do any of the following as well:

- Keep a seasonal log of the land and plant conditions. Whenever you visit your chosen area, write down what you see, smell, hear and feel.

- Plant a small garden there if you can.

- Pull out foreign plants and nurture the native plants.

- Clean up your plant ecosystem at least once every season, or more often if you can do so. Keep a record of what you see and remove. This will help you know what types of pollution or garbage are harming your area and how your efforts are helping. If there is a lot of pollution, get other people to help.

- Ask your friends to get involved. Tell others about what you are doing. Invite them to join you or choose their own plant ecosystems to care for. Call your local newspaper and ask a reporter to write a story about what you are doing and how people can help their plant ecosystems. Use your work to help educate people to take care of ecosystems.

START A GARDEN CLUB

Bring your friends together to create a joint garden. Prepare the land, plant, weed and harvest together. Get a grown-up to help. It doesn't have to be a large area. Choose a reasonable size which you and your friends can manage yourselves.

RECYCLE

Recycle glass, plastic, tin, papers (colored, white and shiny), newspapers, paper bags and batteries. Get your family, friends and neighborhood to recycle. You can earn money doing this. Recycling saves resources (trees, oil, coal, etc. — the soil) and reduces garbage pollution.

USE THE INFORMATION YOU GATHER

Ask your school if you can create a bulletin board to display information about plants and their ecosystems. Include articles from newspapers and magazines, maps and pictures of people doing useful things to protect and propagate plants and their ecosystems.

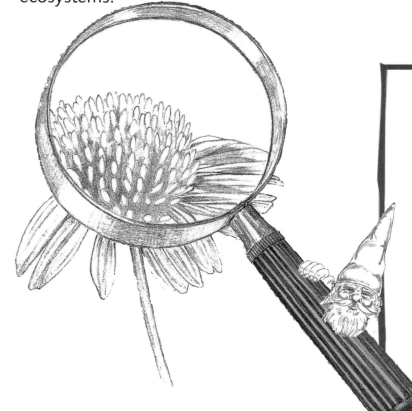

STUDY THE HEALING USES OF YOUR LOCAL PLANTS

Read books, attend lectures or classes, research the library for information and identification, talk to friends and neighbors to learn how plants have helped them. Visit an herbalist or folk healer.

Goodbye!

Kids, Isn't it fun to learn about herbs? There is so much you can make and do with herbs. Did you drink lemon balm tea? have a chamomile bath? eat candied ginger? use mullein oil ear drops? Did you color in all the herb pictures, read all the stories and sing all the songs? What was your favorite story? your favorite song?

Did you put together your own first aid kit? make a salad of edible flowers? have an herbal tea party? plant a garden?

Where did you find **me** throughout this book? (Hint - Look at the bottom of this page.)

I hope you continue learning about herbs and exploring the plants around you. Nature has a lot to share and teach us. Be sure to look for me, too—I'll be close by! Being around plants is one of my favorite places!

Goodbye!

Mr. Greenleaf

(Where I'm hiding in this book: front and back covers, pages 15, 17, 19, 41, 45, 47, 51, 62, 64, 65, 71, 77, 78, 85, 88, 95, 100, 106, 109, 114, 118, 120, 126, 128, 131, 138, 139, 146, 148, 149, 156, 159, 160, 168, 169, 174, 176, 182, 188, 191, 194, 195, 196, 199, 205, 209, 211, 212, 219, 221, 223, 225, 226, 232, 233, 234, 236, 237, 238, 245)

Glossary

Antibiotic *(an-tie-by-ah-tic)* - A substance which fights infections and inflammations.

Bitters - A drink made of bitter-tasting herbs that aids the digestion.

Bruising herbs - Rubbing herbs between your hands to break them up. This helps make their medicine more available.

Capsules *(cap-sols)* - Clear gelatin "containers" which hold powdered herbs and are an easy way to take herbs. The capsules run in different sizes from the small "0", to the medium "00" and the large "000".

Chai *(ch-eye)* - A traditional herbal drink from India that uses kitchen spices; it is also healing.

Chapparral *(shap-are-rel)* - A shrub with tiny yellow flowers; its other names are greasewood and *Larrea tridentata*. It is also the name of any region of the country where shrubs and small trees grow and there are mild, moist winters and hot, dry summers.

Club Moss - This plant is actually not a moss but one of a group of plants related to ferns and horsetail.

Compress - A method of putting herbs on the outside of the body to treat swellings, pains, colds and flus. Herbs that are too strong to be taken inside the body can be put on the outside and the body will absorb a small amount slowly.

Congee *(con-gee)* - A soupy rice porridge made with herbs.

Conifer *(con-ih-fur)* - This is a large group of trees or shrubs that bears its seeds in cones. Examples include cedars, cypresses, firs, hemlocks, junipers, larches, pines, redwoods, sequoias and yews.

Cooling Energy - The special energy of an herb that cools down the body.

Culinary Herb - An herb used in cooking to flavor food and make it tasty.

Decoction *(de-cock-sion)* - A tea made by simmering herbs in water for 10-30 minutes. This form of making tea is used for sturdy plant parts, such as coarse leaves, stems, roots, barks and seeds.

Dream Pillow - A pouch of herbs placed under the pillow or by the nose while sleeping to invite dreams.

Ear Drops - An herbal oil placed in the ear to relieve earaches and ear infections.

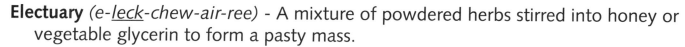

Ecosystem - An area where certain living things come together to feed each other.

Electuary *(e-leck-chew-air-ree)* - A mixture of powdered herbs stirred into honey or vegetable glycerin to form a pasty mass.

Energy of an Herb - The cooling or warming nature of an herb. Cooling herbs cool the body down. Warming herbs warm the body up. This is a natural characteristic of an herb.

Essential Oil - The oil of a flower that holds its scent.

Extract *(x-tract)* - A process of drawing out the effective parts of plants into some form of liquid, either water, glycerin, vinegar, oil or alcohol. Officially an herbal extract is in a concentration of 1-10 or 1-15. This means 1 part of herb makes 10 to 15 parts of extract.

Eyewash - A cooled herbal tea used to rinse the eyes. This heals red, sore eyes, styes and eye infections.

Fomentation *(foe-men-tay-shun)* - A type of compress in which a cloth is soaked in an herb tea, wrung out and then placed directly on the skin. Use it for sore throats, muscle aches and pains, low back pain, cramps and to improve blood circulation.

Foot Bath - A hot herbal bath in which to soak your feet. It warms the feet and whole body, relaxes and eases sore and aching feet.

Foot Powder - Powdered herbs sprinkled on the feet to heal sores, wounds and itching, or to make feet smell pleasing.

Gargle - An herbal tea gargled in the throat to heal sore throats and throat infections.

Glycerite *(glih-sir-ite)* - An herbal extract (tincture) made with glycerin.

Gomasio *(go-mas-e-o)* - Toasted sesame seeds and salt ground together and used in food as a healing seasoning.

Herb - Any plant that is used for healing.

Herbal Bath - A bath which contains herbal tea or herbs.

Herbal Milk - Milk to which an herb, such as cinnamon, has been added for taste and healing.

Infusion *(in-fuse-sion)* - A method of making herbal teas by pouring boiling water over herbs in a pot and letting them steep for 10-15 minutes. It is used for delicate plant parts, such as flowers and soft leaves.

Juice - The liquid extracted from a plant's flowers, fruit, leaves or root.

Liniment *(lynn-a-ment)* - An herbal extract made with alcohol. It is rubbed on the outside of the body into the skin for treating strained muscles and ligaments, bruises, arthritis, some inflammations and cramps.

Lozenge *(la-zenge)* - A tablet or pill that is sucked to ease sore throats or coughs.

Mash - A mushy mixture of herbs created by blending herbs with water until a thick mass is formed.

Massage - Rubbing oil on the body to ease sore muscles, aches and pains, or to relax and ease the body.

Mouthwash - An herbal tea or tincture swished around in the mouth, usually after brushing the teeth. It heals gum infections and gives a nice smell to the breath.

Oils - Herbal extracts made with oil. Some oils can be put in the ears, others are rubbed on the skin for relaxation, to ease sore and strained muscles and joints, or to heal sores, cuts, wounds, rashes or skin eruptions.

Paste - A mixture of herbs with honey that is eaten. This form of taking herbs is delicious and easy to take.

Pill - Powdered herbs mixed with a small binder, such as slippery elm, to hold the herbs together. They are pea-sized and either swallowed or sucked on.

Plaster - Herbs mashed up with water and put on a protective piece of cloth. The cloth is then put directly on the skin. Used for fevers, inflammations, infections, skin eruptions, pain, pus, muscle spasms and internal congestion (such as mucus).

Potherb - Any plant whose leaves are cooked and eaten.

Potpourri (*po-pour-e*) - A mixture of dried herbs that is sweet or spicy smelling and pretty to look at in a bowl or jar.

Poultice (*pole-tice*) - A mashed or steamed herb that is placed directly on the skin. It is then held in place with a bandage. Used for bites, stings, slivers, skin eruptions, inflammations, infections and pain.

Powder - Ground-up herbal parts, such as leaves, barks, twigs or roots, made into a fine powder. This is then mixed in water, milk or honey, put in a capsule or made into a pill to take as medicine.

Sachet (*sah-shay*) - A mixture of sweet or spicy smelling dried herbs that are wrapped in a cloth. They are usually hung in closets or placed in dresser drawers to scent clothes.

Salve - A hardened herbal oil that is rubbed on the skin and left there. Used for bites, stings, cuts, sores, scrapes, burns and other skin problems.

Spice - A plant used in cooking to flavor food.

Steams - Hot steamy air scented with herbs and inhaled. This penetrates the lungs and nostrils, opening the breathing passages.

Steeping - See infusion

Sun tea - Tea made by setting a glass jar full of herbs and water in the sun. This method uses the heat from the sun rather than the stove to make the tea.

Syrup - A thick herbal tea with honey added so it coats the throat and brings out mucus from the lungs. Used for sore throats and coughs.

Tincture - An herbal extract made with glycerin, vinegar or alcohol. The liquid pulls, or extracts, the medicinal properties out of an herb, resulting in the tincture. Officially a tincture is in concentrations of 1-10 or 1-15 parts of herbs to tincture. That is, 1 part herb makes 10 or 15 parts tincture.

Tooth Powder - A powdered herbal mixture used to brush the teeth. It whitens and cleans teeth and heals gum infections.

Warming Energy - The special energy of an herb that warms up the body.

Wash - An herbal tea that is used to wash certain parts of the body to heal various complaints.

Weed - Any plant that is growing where you don't want it to grow.

Appendix 1
Herbs and Their Energies

Every herb has a special energy. The energy of an herb is how it affects the body. Some herbs cool the body down, others warm it up. This happens whether the herb is cold from the refrigerator or hot from the stove, because it is a natural characteristic of the herb. The energy of an herb can never be changed because it was created this way, just as a dog can't become a cat, nor a flower a rock.

HOW TO TELL THE ENERGY OF AN HERB

Here are several ways to learn the energy of an herb:

- See how you feel after eating it: Do you feel warmer? cooler?

- Look at its color: In general, blue, purple and dark-colored plants usually have a cool energy; red, yellow, orange and pink-colored plants usually have a warm energy.

- See how it affects the body: Herbs which calm, lower fevers and cause us to go to the bathroom usually have a cool energy; herbs which stimulate the circulation, give us energy, or make us feel warmer generally have a warm energy.

- Look it up in a book: Sometimes we can't tell the energy of an herb easily. Experts have determined the energy of many herbs for us and we can look at their books. See Resources for suggestions.

- Herbs with a heating energy that warm the body up also heal illnesses with signs of coldness. The box, "Cold Illnesses," gives the signs of coldness.

- Herbs with a cooling energy that cool the body down also heal illnesses with signs of heat. The box, "Hot Illnesses," gives the signs of heat.

- Herbs with a neutral energy neither warm the body up nor cool the body down. Thus, they can be used for either cold illnesses or hot illnesses.

Hot Illnesses

If you have an illness with a hot energy, many of the following signs can appear:

- a red face
- loud voice, talkative
- active, restless, excitable
- sleeping little
- bedcovers thrown off at night
- aggressive or irritable attitude
- warm skin temperature, hands and feet feel hot
- few clothes worn or desired
- sweats easily
- high fever, slight chills
- thirsty, dry mouth
- strong appetite
- scanty urination of a dark yellow color
- constipation with strong-smelling stools that are possibly hard and dry
- bad breath
- preference for cooling foods and drinks

Cold Illnesses

If you have an illness with a cold energy, many of the following signs can appear:

- a pale face
- soft-spoken voice, untalkative
- tired, weak, thin, quiet
- sleeping a lot
- sleeping under lots of bedcovers
- submissive attitude
- cold skin temperature, hands and feet feel cold
- many clothes worn or desired
- little sweating
- low fever, strong chills
- no thirst, wet mouth
- poor appetite
- copious urination of a pale light color
- loose stools or diarrhea; little odor
- breath has little odor
- preference for warm foods and drinks

The following lists the herbs in this book and their energies:

Herb	Energy
Calendula	warm
Cayenne	hot
Chamomile	neutral
Cinnamon	warm
Comfrey	cool
Dandelion	cool
Echinacea	cool
Elder	cool
Fennel	warm
Garlic	warm
Ginger	warm
Lemon Balm	cool
Licorice	neutral
Mullein	cool
Plantain	cool
Slippery elm	neutral
Yarrow	warm

Appendix 2
Doses for Children

Children need a smaller amount of herbs to heal than adults. A convenient rule of thumb for figuring herb dosages for children ages 0-12 is to calculate a fraction of the adult dosage proportionate to the child's body weight. Here is a chart that helps to explain dosage:

$$\frac{\text{Child's weight in pounds}}{150 \text{ pounds}} = \text{the fraction of the adult dose to use}$$

For example, if a child weighs 75 pounds then:

$$\frac{75}{150} = \frac{1}{2}$$

Use 1/2 the amount of the adult dose for a child who weighs 75 pounds. If the adult dose is 2 capsules, then the child's dose is 1/2 of 2 capsules, or 1 capsule. If the adult dose is 1 cup of tea, then the child's dose is a half cup of tea.

Clark's Rule, a standing formula for prescribing children's doses, generally summarizes this:

Weight	Herb Tea
Up to 5 pounds	1 tablespoon
5-15 pounds	2 tablespoons
16-35 pounds	1/4 cup
36-65 pounds	1/2 cup
66-80 pounds	3/4 cup
81-110 pounds	1 cup (adult dose)

A good way to give herbs to infants and children ages 1-3 is to put the herbal tea into a dropper bottle. Then give several dropperfuls of the tea throughout the day. Herbal pills are also easy for children to take. They store well and can be easily carried on trips.

Herbal preparation	Standard Adult Dose
Bitters	1 dropperful, 3 times a day
Capsule	2 capsules, 3 times a day
Ear drops	10 drops in ear, 5-6 times a day
Herbal milk	1 cup, 3 times a day
Pills	2-4 pills, 3 times a day
Powder	1 teaspoon, 3 times a day
Syrup	1 tablespoon, 3-6 times a day
Tea	1 cup, 3 times a day
Tincture	1 dropperful, 3 times a day (or 1 dropperful 6-8 times a day for acute conditions)

Note: a bath, eyewash, fomentation, gargle, liniment, milk decoction, mouthwash, oil, paste, plaster, potherb, poultice, salve, gruel, soup, tooth powder, foot powder, steam or wash is applied or taken as needed for both children and adults.

Appendix 3
A Quick Guide to Treating Illnesses

The following symptoms are those mentioned in this book. After each symptom the herbs which best help that problem are listed. Again, only those herbs discussed in this book are named. Some herbs are more specific for that symptom than others and these are starred(*).

The herbs are listed according to their cooling, neutral and warming inner natures. This should make it easier to decide which of the listed herbs to use. Be sure to find out if the symptom is one of heat or coldness first. Refer to Appendix 1 and see the Hot and Cold Nature of Illness to help you do this.

How do you know which herb to use? There are three clues:

*   First, choose the herb according to its energy. Use cooling herbs to treat illnesses of heat, and warming herbs to treat illnesses of coldness. (Refer to Appendix 1 for more information on the energy of herbs.)

*   Choose whichever herb is easiest to find. Is it growing in your yard? Do you already have it in your kitchen? If you don't have any of the herbs on hand, then which one can you easily find to buy?

*   Look up all the suggested herbs for the illness and see which one most closely matches all of the symptoms being experienced.

Once you choose an herb (or herbs), then look it up in Chapter 2 to see in what form to take it for that symptom. For example, in some cases a tea will work better, in others, a tincture or plaster.

The following represent some traditional uses of the herbs described in this book. These suggestions are not intended to replace proper medical care.

Symptoms	Herbal Remedy		
	Cool	Neutral	Warm
Abdominal pain			cinnamon, ginger
Appetite:			
Loss of			cayenne, cinnamon, ginger
Too much	dandelion	chamomile	
Asthma	plantain, elder	licorice, mullein	garlic, ginger
Bee stings	*echinacea, *plantain, comfrey	licorice, mullein	ginger
Bladder infections	plantain		
Bleeding: (If severe, call a doctor.)			
External		*yarrow	*cayenne, calendula
Internal		*yarrow	
Blood poisoning: (Seek appropriate medical care!)	dandelion, echinacea		
Boils	comfrey, plantain	yarrow	
Broken and fractured bones	*comfrey (externally)	chamomile	
Bronchitis	*elder, plantain	licorice, mullein, slippery elm	*garlic, calendula, ginger
Bug bites	comfrey, echinacea, plantain		
Burns	comfrey, echinacea, elder, plantain	yarrow	calendula
Chicken pox	dandelion, echinacea	yarrow	
Colic		chamomile	cinnamon, ginger
Coldness			cinnamon, garlic, ginger, a little cayenne
Colds	lemon balm	chamomile, licorice, mullein, yarrow	cayenne, cinnamon, garlic, raw ginger
Constipation	plantain, dandelion		

Symptoms	Herbal Remedy		
	Cool	Neutral	Warm
Cough	*elder, lemon balm	*mullein, licorice, slippery elm, yarrow	*garlic, *ginger, cinnamon
Cramps	lemon balm	chamomile, licorice	calendula, cayenne, cinnamon, garlic, ginger
Crying and whining	lemon balm	licorice	chamomile
Cuts	comfrey, echinacea, elder, plantain	chamomile wash, yarrow	calendula
Depression	lemon balm	chamomile, licorice	cayenne
Diaper rash	plantain	slippery elm	calendula
Diarrhea	plantain	mullein, slippery elm, yarrow	cinnamon, cayenne
Digestion, aids	dandelion	chamomile, yarrow	*ginger, cinnamon, cayenne, garlic
Dysentery	plantain	mullein, slippery elm, yarrow	cayenne, cinnamon
Earache/ ear infections	echinacea	*mullein oil, chamomile	calendula oil, garlic
Eczema	dandelion	yarrow	calendula
Energy: low	cayenne, cinnamon, ginger		
Eyes: red and sore	dandelion	yarrow	calendula
Fever	echinacea, elder, lemon balm	yarrow	calendula, raw ginger
Flu	*elder, echinacea, lemon balm	licorice, mullein, yarrow	calendula, cinnamon, garlic, raw ginger
Gall stones	dandelion root		
Gas		chamomile	cinnamon, ginger

Symptoms	Herbal Remedy		
	Cool	Neutral	Warm
Glandular problems		licorice	
Headache	dandelion		cayenne, cinnamon, raw ginger
Hemorrhoids	comfrey (externally) plantain	mullein, yarrow	calendula, ginger
Hepatitis	dandelion, echinacea, plantain		
Herbs to eat as foods	dandelion leaves, elder flowers and berries		cayenne, cinnamon, garlic, ginger
Immunization, effects of	echinacea		
Indigestion	dandelion	chamomile, yarrow	cayenne, cinnamon, garlic, ginger
Infections	*echinacea, plantain; comfrey externally	yarrow	
Inflammations	*echinacea, plantain	yarrow	
Intestinal ulcer	plantain	licorice	calendula
Itching from insect bites	echinacea, plantain		
Joint pains		chamomile wash	cayenne, calendula wash, cinnamon liniment, ginger packs
Kidney infection	plantain		
Low back pain			cinnamon, ginger
Lung problems	*elder, plantain	*mullein, licorice	*garlic, calendula, ginger
Measles	dandelion, plantain	mullein, yarrow	calendula

Symptoms	Herbal Remedy		
	Cool	Neutral	Warm
Mucus: Excessive	*elder	*mullein	*garlic, cinnamon, ginger
Irritated membranes		licorice	
Muscles, sore		chamomile	calendula, cayenne ginger
Nausea		chamomile, slippery elm	*ginger, cinnamon
Nerve pain		chamomile, licorice	
Nervousness	lemon balm	chamomile, licorice	
Nosebleeds		yarrow	
Pain: Abdominal		chamomile	*ginger, calendula, cayenne
Cramps	lemon balm	chamomile, licorice	*ginger, calendula, cinnamon, garlic,
Low back			calendula, ginger
Muscle		chamomile	cayenne
Parasites			garlic
Pneumonia (Seek appropriate medical care.)	elder, lemon balm	licorice, mullein, yarrow	cayenne, cinnamon, garlic, raw ginger
Poison oak and ivy	*plantain, echinacea, dandelion	yarrow	
Rashes	dandelion, echinacea	chamomile, slippery elm	
Red and sore eyes	chamomile, dandelion	yarrow	calendula
Skin problems	echinacea, elder, dandelion, plantain	slippery elm, yarrow	calendula
Skin tears	*comfrey, echinacea, elder, plantain	chamomile, slippery elm, yarrow	calendula
Snake bites (Seek appropriate medical care.)	*echinacea, dandelion		

Symptoms	Herbal Remedy		
	Cool	Neutral	Warm
Sores	comfrey, echinacea, elder, plantain	chamomile, slippery elm, yarrow	calendula
Sore throat	*echinacea, elder	*licorice, *slippery elm	*raw and dry ginger, garlic
Splinters and slivers: draw out	*plantain, comfrey		
Sprains	comfrey (externally)		calendula, cayenne, ginger
Stomachache	dandelion	licorice, yarrow	cinnamon, raw or dry ginger
Stones:			
Gall	dandelion		
Kidney	*dandelion, plantain		
Stress	lemon balm	chamomile, licorice	
Sunburn	plantain	mullein, slippery elm	
Swollen glands	echinacea, elder	slippery elm, yarrow	ginger
Teething	lemon balm, echinacea	licorice	
Thirst		licorice	
Toothaches	echinacea	yarrow	cayenne
Ulcers:			
Stomach	plantain	licorice, slippery elm	calendula
Intestinal		dandelion, plan	ppery elm
Urination:			
Increases	dandelion, plantain		
Vaccination:			
Effects of & reactions to	echinacea		
Vomiting		chamomile, slippery elm	ginger
Whooping cough	lemon balm	licorice, mullein, yarrow	cinnamon, ginger
Wounds	comfrey, echinacea, elder, plantain	slippery elm, yarrow	calendula

Appendix 4
State Flowers and Trees

ach state has chosen a special flower and tree to represent it. Usually it is a flower or tree native to the state, growing readily and abundantly in that area.

What is your state flower and tree?

State	Flower	Tree
Alabama	Camellia	Southern pine (longleaf pine)
Alaska	Forget-me-not	Sitka spruce
Arizona	Saguaro (giant cactus)	Paloverde
Arkansas	Apple blossom	Pine
California	Golden poppy	Redwood
Colorado	Rocky Mountain columbine	Blue spruce
Connecticut	Mountain laurel	White oak
Delaware	Peach blossom	American holly
Florida	Orange	Cabbage palm
Georgia	Cherokee rose	Live oak
Hawaii	Hibiscus	Kukui
Idaho	Syringa (mock orange)	Western white pine
Illinois	Native violet	White oak
Indiana	Peony	Tulip tree (yellow poplar)
Iowa	Wild rose	Oak
Kansas	Sunflower	Cottonwood
Kentucky	Goldenrod	Kentucky coffee tree
Louisiana	Magnolia	Bald cypress
Maine	White pine cone and tassel	White pine
Maryland	Black-eyed Susan	White oak (Wye oak)
Massachusetts	Mayflower	American elm

State	Flower	Tree
Michigan	Apple blossom	White pine
Minnesota	Pink and white lady's slipper	Norway, or red, pine
Mississippi	Magnolia	Magnolia
Missouri	Hawthorn	Flowering dogwood
Montana	Bitterroot	Ponderosa pine
Nebraska	Goldenrod	Cottonwood
Nevada	Sagebrush	Single-leaf pinon
New Hampshire	Purple lilac	White birch
New Jersey	Purple violet	Red oak
New Mexico	Yucca flower	Pinon, or nut pine
New York	Rose	Sugar maple
North Carolina	Flowering dogwood	Pine
North Dakota	Wild prairie rose	American elm
Ohio	Scarlet carnation	Buckeye
Oklahoma	Mistletoe	Redbud
Oregon	Oregon grape	Douglas fir
Pennsylvania	Mountain laurel	Hemlock
Rhode Island	Violet	Red maple
South Carolina	Carolina jessamine (jasmine)	Palmetto
South Dakota	American pasqueflower	Black Hills spruce
Tennessee	Iris	Tulip poplar
Texas	Bluebonnet	Pecan
Utah	Sego lily	Blue spruce
Vermont	Red clover	Sugar maple
Virginia	Dogwood	Dogwood
Washington	Coast rhododendron	Western hemlock
West Virginia	Rhododendron	Sugar maple
Wisconsin	Wood violet	Sugar maple
Wyoming	Indian paintbrush	Cottonwood

Appendix 5
Resources

World-class herbalist training with the
EAST WEST SCHOOL OF PLANETARY HERBOLOGY

Come learn from the best and become the best.

The East West School of Planetary Herbology offers correspondence courses to train home herbalists, health professionals and clinical herbal practitioners. Here you can learn from two of the world's most respected and influential herbalists, alternative health pioneer and American Herbalist Guild founder, Dr. Michael Tierra, O.M.D., and clinical herbalist/acupuncturist, Lesley Tierra, L.Ac., AHG.

Our herbal training course is the only one that teaches Planetary Herbology, a unique approach to herbal medicine that integrates plants and diagnostic tools from the three major healing traditions of the world. Staffed by a talented faculty of professional herbalists, the East West Herbal Correspondence Course offers its students distance and on-site education from the very best experts in the filed. They really do learn from the best and become the best!

> *The credibility of graduating from the program also has great respect nation-wide. I have not walked into a health food store or met an herbalist who wasn't familiar with Michael Tierra. It adds a great deal of credibility when people find out you have studied with him in California.*
> *Nicholas Schnell, Clinical Herbalist, Nutritionist, RD, LMNT.*

Since its founding in 1980, the East West School of Planetary Herbology has graduated the largest number of leaders in the herbal industry and has thousands of students around the world. Our herbalist training offers several levels of in-depth training courses along with supplemental books, CDs, DVDs, webinars, weekly chats, and a private student discussion forum.

For more information contact the East West School of Planetary Herbology:
website: www.planetherbs.com   email: herbcourse@planetherbs.com
P.O. Box 275 Ben Lomond CA 95005
831-336-5010   800-717-5010

BOOKS ON HERBS (Adult)

Lust, John and Tierra, Michael, *The Natural Remedy Bible*, Pocket Books, 1990.

Romm, Aviva Jill and Sears, William, *Natural Health for Babies and Children*, Crossing Press 1996.

Tierra, Lesley, *Healing with the Herbs of Life*, Crossing Press, 2004.

Tierra, Michael, *The Way of Herbs*, Pocket Books, 1998.

Tierra, Michael, *Planetary Herbology*, Lotus Press, 1988.

Tompkins, Peter and Bird, *The Secret Life of Plants*, Harper Colophon Books, 1973.

NOVELS FOR KIDS WHO LOVE HERBS

Atnip, Linda, *Miranda's Magic Garden*, BlueStar Communications, 1997.

Bear, Walking Night and Stan Padilla, *Song of the Seven Herbs*, Book Publishing Co., 1987.

Carter, Forrest, *The Education of Little Tree*, University of New Mexico Press, 1990.

Cushman, Karen, *The Midwife's Apprentice*, Clarion Books, 1995.

de la Tour, Shatoiya, *The Herbalist of Yarrow*, Tzedakah Publications, 1994.

Fleishman, Paul, *Seedfolks*, HarperCollins Children's Books, 1997.

Furlong, Monica, *Juniper,* Random House, 1992.

Furlong, Monica, *Wise Child*, Random House, 1982.

Hardin, Jesse Wolf, *I'm a Mediciine Woman, Too!*, HOPS Press, 2009

Hart, Avery and Paul Mantell, *Kids Garden!*, Williamson Publishing Company, 1996.

Strichartz, Naomi, *The Wisewoman*, Cranehill Press, 1986.

FLOWER WISDOM AND CRAFTS

Diamond, Denise, *Living with Flowers*, Quill, 1982.

HERB GAME

Wildcraft! An Herbal Adventure Game, a cooperative board game by LearningHerbs for ages 4 and up.

GROWING HERBS (Adult)

Foster, Steven, *Herbal Bounty*, Peregrine Smith Books, 1984.

LIVE HERBS AND SEEDS

Mountain Rose Herbs: www.mountainroseherbs.com/catalog/home-goods/seeds; P.O. Box 50220 Eugene OR 97405; (800) 879-3337

Sustainable Seed Company: 877-620-SEED

Horizon Herbs: P.O. Box 69 Williams OR 97544; 541-846-6704; www.horizonherbs.com

Pacific Botanicals: 4840 Fish Hatchery Road, Grants Pass OR 97527; www.pacificbotanicals.com

Starwest Botanicals: 161 Main Ave Sacramento CA 95838; (800) 800-4372; International: (916) 638-8100; www.starwest-botanicals.com

HERB SUPPLIERS

Herbalist and Alchemist, Inc.: 51 South Wandling Ave. Washington NJ 07882; 908-689-9020; www.herbalist-alchemist.com

Herb Pharm: PO Box 116 Williams OR 97544; 800-348-4372;

www.herb-pharm.com

Organic Connections: 877-899-3736; www.orgcon.ca (Canada)

Planetary Herbals: P.O. Box 275 Ben Lomond CA 95005; 831-336-5010; 800-717-5010; www.planetherbs.com; herbcourse@planetherbs.com

Index to Herbal Stories

Index to Songs

General Index

About the Author

Lesley Tierra is a California State and nationally certified Acupuncturist (L. Ac.) and Herbalist. She has a practice in Santa Cruz, California where she combines acupuncture, herbs and food therapies along with lifestyle and inner growth counseling. She is a founding and professional member of the American Herbalist Guild (AHG).

Lesley is the author of *Healing With The Herbs of Life* (Crossing Press, 2004), *Healing with Chinese Herbs* (Crossing Press, 1997), and co-author of *Chinese Traditional Herbal Medicine Volumes I and II* with Michael Tierra (Lotus Press, 1998). She collaborated with Michael Tierra to produce the East West Herb Course and is its Dean.

Lesley has taught Chinese healing theory and techniques, herbology and women's groups at various schools, seminars and symposiums throughout the United States and England since 1983. She has also taught children Red Cross Swimming, synchronized swimming and, through the Artists in the Schools program in Wyoming, photography.

About the Artist

Susie Wilson is an English artist who has resided in the United States for the past ten years. Originally trained as a fine artist, she worked for several years as a college lecturer in Europe. At the same time she gained a considerable reputation for portraits and botanical studies in pastel, pencil and watercolour and for her unusual style of faux finishes and mural art.

She now enjoys a successful career as a illustrator and art director, counting amongst her clients Paramount Studios, Broderbund, Tsunami Media, "Babylon 5" science fiction series, Discovery Channel and the San Francisco Zoo. Recently, Susie has produced a range of greeting cards and address books which are distributed world wide.

Hey Kids!
Follow Mr. Greenleaf to the Magical World of Herbs!

JOIN THE KIDS HERBAL FAMILY CLUB!

What's waiting for you –

1) Pictures of herbs
2) Songs and stories
3) Collectable herbal trading cards

To sign up, follow Mr. Greenleaf to:
planetherbs.com/magicalherbs
for all of this plus more herbal fun!

YOUNG ADULTS, MOMS, DADS, TEACHERS, AND OTHER ADULTS:

The Kids Herbal Family Club is a stepping stone to becoming a naturopath, physician, herbalist, acupuncturist, botanist, scientist, or other professional. Help them join today!

ALSO GO TO: planetherbs.com, click on the "Courses" tab and then the "Home Herbalist Course" to learn about the next level of herbal studies for this child – and for you!